Editorial Project Manager
Erica N. Russikoff, M.A.

Editor in Chief
Karen J. Goldfluss, M.S. Ed.

Creative Director
Sarah M. Fournier

Cover Artist
Sarah Kim

Imaging
Amanda R. Harter

Publisher
Mary D. Smith, M.S. Ed.

KNOW T...
Mastering
Academic Vocabulary

- Introduces a variety of strategies that help students learn the language of the classroom
- Provides practice with need-to-know academic vocabulary used in all subjects
- Improves students' ability to understand and follow directions
- Includes Lexile measures and standards correlations

Teacher Created Resources

Author
Tracie I. Heskett, M. Ed.

Teacher Created Resources
12621 Western Avenue
Garden Grove, CA 92841
www.teachercreated.com
ISBN: 978-1-4206-8135-2
© 2018 Teacher Created Resources
Made in U.S.A.

Teacher Created Resources

TABLE OF CONTENTS

INTRODUCTION

In order for students to acquire new knowledge and learning, they must be able to understand what they read, hear, and are asked to do in the classroom. According to Robert Marzano, a leading researcher in education and author of several books on academic vocabulary, students must comprehend academic vocabulary in order to understand instruction and academic texts. Often, students have a hard time writing to prompts or responding to instructions because they don't know exactly what is being asked. This is because they don't understand the meanings behind instructional verbs or how these words are used in an academic context.

What Is Academic Vocabulary?

Academic vocabulary is the language of the classroom. It includes academic language—the specific words and phrases that students encounter in their academic reading, assignments, and daily classroom activities—as well as the grammar and language structures that make up classroom discussions. Academic vocabulary incorporates words not always used in everyday conversation, and sentences may be more complex. In some cases, students encounter words that have different meanings than they do in other contexts.

Academic vocabulary refers to words and phrases that are used in the process of learning. Benjamin Bloom, an educational psychologist, worked with colleagues to create and publish a taxonomy that provides a framework for classroom instruction. Bloom's Taxonomy has been updated to reflect the action words students encounter in their learning while maintaining a hierarchy of higher-order thinking. Each level contains key words found in academic tasks for that level of critical thinking. Current standards emphasize the need for students to develop critical-thinking skills. Bloom's Taxonomy labels the levels of higher-order thinking as remembering, understanding, applying, analyzing, evaluating, and creating.

Teachers and students use academic language to discuss new knowledge and concepts, develop ideas, talk about texts, and engage in classroom activities. This book will focus on terms used specifically in classroom instruction. Many of these terms are included in Bloom's Taxonomy, which enables teachers to identify objectives and plan instruction that develop critical-thinking skills and to assess student learning. Direct instruction in academic vocabulary supports students by helping them understand what they are expected to do.

This book contains three main components: strategies to help teachers explain academic vocabulary; lessons that present definitions, examples, and practice of academic instructional verbs; and a glossary, which includes related, non-specific academic language to further develop students' working vocabulary.

HOW TO USE THIS BOOK

Know the Lingo! Mastering Academic Vocabulary contains strategies, specific lessons and activities, and a glossary to help teachers illustrate and teach instructional verbs and other academic vocabulary. Introduce and discuss the concept of academic vocabulary with students. Explain that in school, teachers ask students to do certain things in the classroom. When teachers tell students what to do or how to do something, we call these sentences *instructions* or *directions*. It is important for students to understand what the words used in directions mean, so they will be able to successfully do what is being asked. In these lessons, students will learn the meanings of words teachers use when giving instructions. Other times, students read words that tell them what to do; these are called *written directions.* When first starting these lessons, help students understand the nature of and expected response to a *prompt*. A prompt is a sentence that tells students which action to take. Review also the concept of *task,* meaning a specific piece of work to be done, often assigned by another person. The glossary lists additional academic vocabulary students encounter in the context of instruction, activities, and other classroom materials. Students need to understand the meanings of these words in order to successfully complete academic tasks within the classroom. Copy these pages for students and explain to them that they will keep their glossaries handy to help them understand academic words used in the prompts and tasks in the lessons.

The strategies and examples listed on "Strategies to Teach Academic Vocabulary" (pages 6–7) offer support for students who need additional assistance in making connections between words, their meanings, and expected actions. They may be used with various instructional verbs and other academic vocabulary to teach students and help them incorporate academic vocabulary into their daily learning.

The "Academic Instructional Verbs" section (pages 8–103) highlights grade-appropriate instructional verbs that students will find included in many prompts. These words include *describe*, *indicate*, *evaluate*, and *summarize*. The word list is compiled from grade-level standards and Bloom's Taxonomy. Lessons are presented in an order that correlates to the frequency with which students might encounter the word. For example, most prompts ask students to "report," so that lesson is one of the first taught. Each verb is explained in the following ways:

- **Define:** Students are provided with a definition of the instructional verb.
- **Study:** Students are asked to review sample prompts and tasks that include the instructional verb as well as sample responses to the prompts and tasks.
- **Practice:** Students practice answering prompts and completing tasks that contain the instructional verb.
- **Check:** Students participate in a small-group or whole-class activity to confirm their understanding of the instructional verb.
- **Review:** Students are reminded of how the instructional verb is used.
- **Collaborate:** Students collaborate in pairs to further demonstrate their understanding of the instructional verb.

HOW TO USE THIS BOOK (cont.)

Preview each lesson to ensure you have the needed materials on hand. When this icon appears [✐], prepare or complete the activity as directed. Guide students through the sample prompts and sample answers provided in each lesson to help students understand the meaning of the academic verb. Then preview the practice prompts and tasks to which students will respond. Ensure students have the "Academic Concepts Glossary" (pages 104–108) for reference as they complete individual, whole-class, small-group, or paired activities. Designate a place for students to store their glossaries for easy access during classroom instruction and activities. Sometimes a sample prompt or activity includes a short reading passage for students. Most reading passages fall within the fifth-grade reading range based on Lexile measures (830L–1010L). For further review, consider using this comprehension check format as a follow-up to the lesson activities:

CHECK YOUR WORK

Think about your answers to the following questions. Discuss your thoughts with a partner or other classmates, or write your responses in a journal entry.

- Did you know what to do?
- Was it easy or hard to understand what the word or phrase means?
- Could you tell someone else what to do if they heard this word?
- In your own words, what does this word mean?

Note: Any Common Core State Standards addressed in lesson activities are listed on pages 110–112.

ACADEMIC VOCABULARY NOTEBOOKS

Consider having students keep academic vocabulary notebooks. Notebooks will help students with word recognition in future encounters. Encourage students to refer to their notebooks during various cross-curricular activities.

- Create and maintain a class "journal" to observe and discuss academic vocabulary in practice throughout a school day.
- Have students copy the word and a simple definition for reference in small-group discussions and activities.
- Have students write observations and new information about academic vocabulary.
- Have students write comments about their experiences with academic vocabulary in classroom activities.
- Encourage students to make connections across content areas.
- Have students discuss and compare their observations with classmates.
- Have students compare terms within or between subject areas.
- Provide activities that engage students in using terms from their notebooks.
- Have students edit and revise their notebooks to reflect new learning.

STRATEGIES TO TEACH ACADEMIC VOCABULARY

Each lesson includes specific tasks and strategies to help students learn academic vocabulary. Refer to the following tips to provide additional support for students who have trouble grasping a vocabulary concept.

Strategy	Example
Consider the language expectations in the lesson and text before teaching.	What are students being asked to do in this lesson? What academic vocabulary is embedded in the text?
Check which words students need to know in order to understand any instructions in the lesson.	Underline or highlight academic instructional verbs in the lesson instructions. Check for student understanding before teaching the lesson.
Evaluate what students already know about the terms.	Do they know what the word means? Do they know how to perform the action?
Review words and phrases with students to add to their knowledge base.	Point out different types of responses students make during classroom activities to broaden their understanding of the term.
Make sure students understand the words in directions or assignments.	Read a direction aloud. Ask students to verbally *describe* what they would do to complete that direction, in their own words, if possible.
Model how to use sentence starters to practice completing a writing prompt.	Think aloud to *investigate* the purposes of informational text. The main idea of this piece is _____. In this text, I learned that _____.
Provide pictorial representation with the definition of a word when possible.	Show pictures in a logical order (e.g., morning, noon, and night) to *explain* sequential order.
Provide students with a description, example, or explanation when giving a formal definition of a word or phrase.	Show students a simple diagram to define a word such as *distinguish*: Draw two circles and explain that we can list characteristics of two things or ideas to tell how they are different.
Have students draw a picture or create a symbol or other graphic to represent the term.	Students might draw arrows to help them remember what to do when they *predict* or *indicate*.
Have students state their own descriptions, examples, or explanations.	Ask students to *clarify* what it means to *interpret* an author's purpose, a topic, or the way words are used to convey specific meaning.

STRATEGIES TO TEACH ACADEMIC VOCABULARY *(cont.)*

Strategy	Example
Break objectives and prompts down into parts to guide students.	Break a prompt such as "Use evidence from informational texts to support your analysis, reflection, and research of a topic" into separate questions: What did you find (evidence) in your research to support the new information you have learned about your topic? How did these facts, details, definitions, examples, and reasons (evidence) help you better understand your topic?
Consider having EL students write definitions in their native language.	*describir: explicar con detalle las características de algo o alguien* (to describe: explain with detail the characteristics of something or someone) Compare to our definition: to *describe* means to create a picture of something in words
Incorporate student practice with vocabulary words and language structures during collaborative or independent work.	Have students explore working definitions of a verb such as *arrange* and act out/practice what they have learned.
Have students discuss new terms with each other.	Encourage students to discuss what it means to *evaluate* and give examples of when they have done this.
Include games along with vocabulary activities.	Students may enjoy playing games, such as a matching memory game or a beanbag toss, to learn the meanings of words.
Help students make connections between academic words and what they are expected to do or know how to do.	Consider having students generate a chart listing several instructional verbs with a picture next to each verb illustrating what a student would do to perform that action.
Refer to specific academic vocabulary and its meanings in everyday activities.	If students are making a class decision, ask individuals what they might say to *persuade* classmates to consider their ideas.
Teach language and content together when applicable.	Provide examples of what it means to *report* in a variety of contexts (e.g., science or social studies).
Brainstorm with students ways they could complete a specific prompt or task.	Conduct a class discussion to create a web or chart listing ways students could develop a topic, or how they could include text features and illustrations to increase reader comprehension.

COLLABORATE

DEFINE

Question: What does it mean to <u>collaborate</u>?
Answer: When we <u>collaborate</u>, we work together to do or make something. Often, we <u>collaborate</u> in learning situations.

STUDY

Sample Prompt: Why might people <u>collaborate</u> with others to create a tiny house?
Sample Answer: They can get ideas and learn the best way to do things.

Sample Prompt: How do people <u>collaborate</u> in tiny-house communities?
Sample Answer: They may share cooking facilities or garden space.

PRACTICE

① **Task:** Read the definition of a tiny house below. Then <u>collaborate</u> with a classmate to write a description of a tiny house in your own words.

The tiny-house movement is a trend in which some people live in very small houses. At 400 square feet or less, a tiny house is less than one-fourth the size of an average house and is also less expensive. Some tiny houses are as small as 100 square feet. In such a small space, people live simply with far fewer possessions. A tiny house is very efficient; everything is smaller, and every bit of space counts.

_____

_____

② **Prompt:** What do you think you would or would not like about living in a tiny house?

_____

_____

③ **Task:** Consult with your partner to <u>collaborate</u> and explore the topic of tiny houses. Take notes about your conversation.

_____

_____

④ **Prompt:** What have you learned about <u>collaborating</u> by working with a classmate to complete Practice Tasks #1 and #3?

_____

_____

COLLABORATE (cont.)

☑ CHECK

Look back at what the word <u>collaborate</u> means.

① <u>Collaborate</u> with a small group to learn why people might choose to live in a tiny house.

② Read magazine articles or look at websites to research tiny houses in today's culture. 📝

③ Talk with others in your group about their previous knowledge or experiences with the tiny-house movement.

④ <u>Collaborate</u> to decide which information from your research and discussion would be most important and interesting to include in an overview of tiny-house communities. Take notes on your discoveries.

_____

_____

_____

_____

🔍 REVIEW

- When we <u>collaborate</u>, we work together with others to achieve or do something.
- Often, we <u>collaborate</u> in learning situations.
- Often, when we <u>collaborate</u>, we work together to produce or make something.

🗨 COLLABORATE

When we look back at what this word means, we see that it means to work together with others to do something.

① <u>Collaborate</u> with a partner to design a tiny house. Which features of a tiny house would be most important? Why?

_____

_____

_____

_____

② Use your notes from #1 above, Practice Prompt #2, and Practice Task #3 to explain your ideas as you <u>collaborate</u> to create a diagram of your tiny house. Draw your diagram on a separate piece of paper.

Name: _____

REPORT

 DEFINE

Question: What does it mean to <u>report</u>?

Answer: When we <u>report</u>, we write a detailed statement or tell what happened. We give information or describe our feelings when we <u>report</u> on something.

 STUDY

Sample Prompt: Why do people <u>report</u>?

Sample Answer: People <u>report</u> to communicate information that might be of interest to a particular audience.

Sample Prompt: The government <u>reports</u> on the status of various ecosystems. Why is it important for the government to <u>report</u> this information?

Sample Answer: <u>Reporting</u> on ecosystems helps us to understand what we can do to better help the environment.

 PRACTICE

① **Task:** Read the paragraph below about a desert ecosystem.

Within the desert biome, different ecosystems exist. The oasis is an ecosystem with unique plants and animals. A spring or small pond provides water, which enables plants to grow. Often, an oasis will have palm trees. People who settle in an oasis grow crops such as dates, olives, or corn. It is important to use the fresh water wisely and plant trees carefully to protect the oasis ecosystem from the harsh desert sands.

② **Prompt:** <u>Report</u> on interesting details and information you learned from reading the paragraph in Practice Task #1.

_____

_____

_____

_____

③ **Prompt:** <u>Report</u> your feelings about the topic of the paragraph.

_____

_____

_____

_____

Name: _____

REPORT *(cont.)*

☑ CHECK

Look back at what the word <u>report</u> means.

Use a separate piece of paper to complete this activity. Work together with a small group (at least three students) to research marshlands. Each person in the group will have a different role.

- One or two people will gather facts and information about the topic and <u>report</u> their findings to the group.
- Each person in the group will note details and ideas about the topic that they find most important or interesting.
- One or two people will listen to the group discussion and write what the group decides to <u>report</u> to other classmates.
- Another person will <u>report</u> the group's main ideas to the rest of the class.

🔍 REVIEW

- We <u>report</u> when we say or write what happened.
- When we <u>report</u>, we give a detailed statement about something that happened.
- When we <u>report</u> on something, we give information about it.
- We tell people about something when we <u>report</u>.
- When we <u>report</u>, we might describe our feelings about a thing or event.

💬 COLLABORATE

When we look back at what this word means, we see that it means to say or write details or information about something.

Use a separate piece of paper to complete these activities:

① Work with a classmate to research an ecosystem in your area.

② Collaborate to determine which facts and details best support your ideas about the topic. Take notes with your partner.

③ Include visual aids to make it easier for classmates to understand your ideas.

④ <u>Report</u> to classmates on the topic you researched. Show your visual aid.

Name: _____

EXPLAIN

 ## DEFINE

Question: What does it mean to explain?
Answer: When we explain, we make something clear so that it is easier to understand. We give reasons to tell what it means.

 ## STUDY

Sample Prompt: Explain the need for alternate sources of energy.
Sample Answer: Some sources of energy, such as fossil fuels, are limited. Renewable sources of energy can be used over and over again.

Sample Prompt: Explain why people still use fossil fuels.
Sample Answer: Some renewable sources of energy cost more to produce or are not available in all areas.

 ## PRACTICE

① **Prompt:** What are your thoughts on wind power?

_____

_____

② **Task:** Use printed and online reference materials to learn about wind power. Answer the questions below. Take notes on a separate piece of paper. 🖊

- How does wind power work?
- How do people generate wind power?
- What factors need to be considered to use wind power?
- What are the benefits of using wind power? What is one drawback to using wind power? Give examples to explain your answers.

③ **Prompt:** Use your notes from Practice Prompt #1 and Practice Task #2 to write a clear informative paragraph that explains wind power.

_____

_____

_____

_____

_____

_____

EXPLAIN (cont.)

☑ CHECK

Look back at what the word explain means.

① Work with a small group to choose a form of renewable energy you will explain. Some forms of renewable energy include solar power, hydropower, biomass, biofuel, and geothermal energy. Write your topic below.

We will explain _____.

② Independently, write one or two sentences to explain your understanding of how that form of renewable energy works.

_____

_____

③ Review your ideas with others in your small group. Do additional research on your topic if necessary. [✐]

④ Work together to write a paragraph that explains how your chosen form of renewable energy works. Include reasons to explain why people might choose to use this form of energy. Use a separate piece of paper.

⚲ REVIEW

- We explain something when we make it clear and easy to understand.
- We can explain something by telling what it means.
- We explain something when we give reasons.
- When we explain something, we tell or show the reason for it.

🗫 COLLABORATE

When we look back at what this word means, we see that it means to give reasons to make something easy to understand.

① Read a classmate's response to Practice Prompt #3.

② What are the main ideas your partner explains in his or her writing? Explain how each idea is supported by one or more reasons and details.

_____

_____

③ Discuss with your partner how well he or she explained the topic and relationships between ideas in the piece.

Name: _____

DEVELOP

 DEFINE

Question: What does it mean to <u>develop</u> something?
Answer: When we <u>develop</u> something, we build on an idea. We might add facts, details, and other information to <u>develop</u> a topic. We <u>develop</u> our ideas to make them easier to understand and to strengthen our writing.

 STUDY

Sample Prompt: How does <u>developing</u> our ideas about a topic make our writing stronger and more effective?
Sample Answer: When our ideas are clearly supported by relevant details, our writing will be more interesting to readers.

Sample Prompt: What other information can we use to <u>develop</u> a topic?
Sample Answer: We can use definitions, quotations, and examples related to the topic.

✏️ **PRACTICE**

① **Prompt:** What is your opinion about how recent or current immigration affects our society today?

_____

_____

_____

_____

② **Prompt:** What reasons, facts, and other information could you add to <u>develop</u> your ideas about current immigration?

_____

_____

_____

_____

③ **Prompt:** Which specific details would <u>develop</u> your topic to make it more interesting for others to read?

_____

_____

_____

_____

DEVELOP *(cont.)*

☑ CHECK

Look back at what the word <u>develop</u> means.

① Work with classmates to use an interactive whiteboard or chart paper to create a chart similar to the sample shown below. [✐]

② Complete the chart together as you practice <u>developing</u> ideas about how immigration in the past has affected our culture over time.

Steps to Develop a Topic	Class Responses
Take notes about your experiences and observations regarding the topic.	
Ask questions about the topic.	
Read printed and online information about the topic.	
Identify the author's point of view about the topic, and determine which aspects of his or her opinion you agree or disagree with.	
Explore your connections between the topic and the world, other texts, and people you know.	

🔍 REVIEW

- We <u>develop</u> a subject by adding more information about it.
- We can <u>develop</u> our ideas about a topic by adding more details to make our writing clear and easy to read.
- When we <u>develop</u> our ideas, we make them stronger and more effective.
- We can use facts and information to <u>develop</u> what we want to say.

💬 COLLABORATE

When we look back at what this word means, we see that it means to add more information about a subject.

Use a separate piece of paper to complete these activities:

① Work with a classmate to write a narrative about an experience immigrants might have.

② Discuss how you will <u>develop</u> the real or imagined experience. Will your narrative take place in the present or in the past?

③ How will you <u>develop</u> characters so readers will care and want to read about what happens to them? What details can you include as you write what characters do and say that will help readers visualize them?

④ Which events will you include to <u>develop</u> the story, including a problem characters face and how they solve it?

Name: _____

DESCRIBE

 ## DEFINE

Question: What does it mean to <u>describe</u> something?
Answer: When we <u>describe</u> something, we create a picture with words. We give details about people, places, things, or events. We might <u>describe</u> the characters, setting, and events in a story.

 ## STUDY

Sample Prompt: How can we <u>describe</u> an unusual sport?
Sample Answer: We can use action words and adjectives to <u>describe</u> an unusual sport.

Sample Prompt: What types of details can we include to <u>describe</u> something?
Sample Answer: Answering questions such as who, what, where, when, why, and how can help readers picture the activity or event we are <u>describing</u>.

PRACTICE

① **Task:** View print or online pictures of hot-air balloons and related activities. 📝

② **Task:** Create a story map to brainstorm a narrative about a character's experience with hot-air balloons. Use a separate piece of paper.

③ **Prompt:** How would you <u>describe</u> the character(s) in the story?

_____

_____

_____

④ **Prompt:** Which details would you include to <u>describe</u> the setting of the story?

_____

_____

_____

⑤ **Prompt:** What sensory details could you use to <u>describe</u> events that are part of the hot-air balloon experience?

_____

_____

_____

Name: _____

DESCRIBE *(cont.)*

☑ CHECK

Look back at what the word <u>describe</u> means.

① Work with a small group to write questions, similar to the examples below, about an unusual sport, such as bungee jumping. Use a separate piece of paper.

- How would you <u>describe</u> a picture you have seen of someone bungee jumping?
- Where do people bungee jump? What are some situations in which people bungee jump?
- What equipment do people need to participate in bungee jumping?
- Why do people participate in this sport?

② In your small group or with the whole class, participate in a beanbag-toss activity. 🖊

③ On the first round, as each person receives the beanbag, he or she will say a phrase or sentence to <u>describe</u> his or her answer to one of the questions above about bungee jumping.

④ Play another round of beanbag toss with classmates. This time, <u>describe</u> how you would answer one of the questions you wrote in your small group to <u>describe</u> an unusual sport.

🔍 REVIEW

- To <u>describe</u> something means to create a picture with words.
- We can <u>describe</u> the setting of a story. We can also <u>describe</u> the characters and events in a story.
- When we <u>describe</u>, we give details to tell about something.
- We can <u>describe</u> people, places, things, or events.

💬 COLLABORATE

When we look back at what this word means, we see that it means to create a picture of something with words.

Use a separate piece of paper to complete these activities:

① Work with a partner to read print and online materials to research parasailing. 🖊

② Work together to create an imaginary company that would offer this sport in your area.

③ Use the information you have gathered to brainstorm and list specific words and phrases you would use to <u>describe</u> this sport to interest people in participating in it.

④ Create a brochure for the company to <u>describe</u> and advertise the sport to attract customers. Include concrete words and sensory details to help readers picture the sport <u>described</u>.

⑤ Share your brochure with another pair of classmates.

Name: _____

CHOOSE

DEFINE

Question: What does it mean to <u>choose</u>?

Answer: When we <u>choose</u>, we pick out one thing from two or more things. From among different possibilities, we <u>choose</u> the one we prefer or that is best for the situation. We might <u>choose</u> a thing or an action.

STUDY

Sample Prompt: What are some flavors of popcorn people can <u>choose</u> as a snack?

Sample Answer: Flavors of popcorn include caramel corn, cheesy popcorn, and kettle corn. Some cities also have gourmet popcorn shops that have many different flavors.

Sample Prompt: What is one way people <u>chose</u> to eat popcorn in the past?

Sample Answer: Long ago, people ate popcorn as a breakfast cereal since it is a whole grain.

✏️ PRACTICE

① **Prompt:** If you wanted a healthy snack, would you <u>choose</u> popcorn? Why or why not?

_____

_____

_____

_____

_____

② **Prompt:** What factors would affect when you might <u>choose</u> to have popcorn as a snack?

_____

_____

_____

_____

_____

③ **Prompt:** Which flavor of popcorn would you <u>choose</u> to snack on with friends?

_____

④ **Prompt:** If you were to invent a new flavor of popcorn, which flavor would you <u>choose</u>?

_____

Name: _____

CHOOSE *(cont.)*

☑ CHECK

Look back at what the word <u>choose</u> means.

Use a separate piece of paper to complete these activities:

① Work in a small group to create a survey form to ask classmates which snack food they would <u>choose</u> as their favorite.

② After you survey your classmates, ask and answer questions to understand which snack foods classmates would <u>choose</u> most often or least often.

③ As a group, write one or more opinion statements about the data you collected.

④ As a class, discuss the data and compare with classmates the opinion statements you wrote within your group.

⑤ Participate in a class discussion about who might use information about the snack foods students <u>choose</u> and how they might use this information.

🔍 REVIEW

· We decide from among different possibilities when we <u>choose</u>.

· When we <u>choose</u> something, we pick out the one that is best for the situation.

· When we <u>choose</u> something, we might pick out the one we prefer.

· We can <u>choose</u> or decide on an action.

💬 COLLABORATE

When we look back at what this word means, we see that it means to pick out one thing from two or more different things.

Use a separate piece of paper to complete these activities:

① Work with a partner to create a graphic organizer about when and how people <u>choose</u> healthy snacks. Study print or online images of graphic organizers to <u>choose</u> one that will work best for the information you will present. [✐]

② Include information about different activities people might be doing when they want a healthy snack, such as watching a movie.

③ Ask and answer questions about why people <u>choose</u> a certain snack for different activities and the types of healthy snacks they might <u>choose</u>.

④ Present your graphic organizer to classmates to give them ideas about how to <u>choose</u> healthy snacks for themselves.

Name: _____

PLAN

DEFINE

Question: What does it mean to <u>plan</u>?
Answer: When we <u>plan</u>, we work out ahead of time how we will do something. We <u>plan</u> the parts or details before it happens. When we <u>plan</u> to do something, we expect to do it.

STUDY

Sample Prompt: How would you <u>plan</u> to paint a picture?
Sample Answer: I would determine the subject of my painting, then outline it and think about what kind of paint would be best for the paper and subject.

Sample Prompt: What other things do you need to <u>plan</u> to complete an art project?
Sample Answer: I need to think about which kind of paper would be best to use and what perspective I want to take on the subject. I need to consider how long it will take to finish the picture and how long any paint will take to dry.

PRACTICE

① **Task:** Read the paragraph below.

Famous painter Georgia O'Keeffe believed strongly in drawing as practice for painting. She sketched her experiences and visual perceptions. These drawings became the basis for her to explore new art ideas. She used firm, clear lines to emphasize the forms of a subject. Then the artist outlined each composition on canvas before painting with color.

② **Prompt:** How did the artist <u>plan</u> her work ahead of time?

_____

_____

_____

_____

③ **Prompt:** What did you learn about how to <u>plan</u> an art project from reading this example of how one person <u>planned</u> her work?

_____

_____

_____

_____

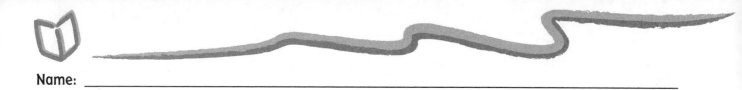

PLAN (cont.)

☑ CHECK

Look back at what the word <u>plan</u> means.

Use a separate piece of paper to complete these activities:

① Work with classmates to <u>plan</u> a mural for your school or community.

② What different things do you need to consider to <u>plan</u> your mural?

③ List the materials you will need for your project.

④ What details do you need to <u>plan</u> to create the mural?

⑤ What role might technology play in the completed project?

⑥ Work together to sketch a design for your mural.

⑦ <u>Plan</u> how you will complete the project, and then create the mural, if possible.

🔍 REVIEW

· When we <u>plan</u> to do something, we mean to do it.

· When we <u>plan</u> something, we think about and arrange the parts or details before it happens or before it is made.

💬 COLLABORATE

When we look back at what this word means, we see that it means to think about and say or write how we will do something.

① Work together with a classmate to <u>plan</u> a collage.

② Discuss how shapes work together to create designs.

③ Determine an overall message or theme for your collage. You might <u>plan</u> to create a design and message about a memorable place in your community. Take notes in the box below.

④ <u>Plan</u> the shapes, colors, and possible images for your collage.

⑤ Create your collage on a separate piece of paper.

⑥ As time allows, present your finished collage to classmates. Invite them to share words that come to mind as they view your art.

PREPARE

📖 DEFINE

Question: What does it mean to prepare?
Answer: When we prepare, we get ready for an activity. We might put together various parts of a whole or plan the details of something.

👤 STUDY

Sample Prompt: How would you prepare to answer a writing prompt?
Sample Answer: I would circle action words that say what the prompt is asking me to do. I would underline descriptive words that help me understand the topic of the prompt.

Sample Prompt: What things do you gather to prepare for a family trip to the store?
Sample Answer: We prepare by writing a list of items to buy, getting out our reusable shopping bags, and bringing any coupons we will use.

✏️ PRACTICE

① **Prompt:** How would you prepare for a family journey? What would you do?

_____

_____

_____

_____

② **Prompt:** Which details would you think about to prepare for such a journey?

_____

_____

_____

③ **Prompt:** How would you prepare to write about an experience you had of taking a journey?

_____

_____

_____

_____

PREPARE *(cont.)*

☑ CHECK

Look back at what the word <u>prepare</u> means.

① <u>Prepare</u> for a class discussion by thinking and reading about what you already know about class field trips.

② Participate in a class discussion about a field trip your class might take.

Use a separate piece of paper to complete these activities:

③ <u>Prepare</u> notes about what you need to do before going on the class field trip.

④ <u>Prepare</u> to write about what you expect on the class field trip. Choose one of the following pre-writing options:

- Create a story map.
- Brainstorm using a web.
- Outline your ideas.
- Cluster your thoughts and make connections between them and new ideas.
- Do a freewriting exercise.

⑤ As time allows, write a paragraph about what you expect would happen on a class field trip based on how you and your classmates <u>prepared</u> for the trip.

⚲ REVIEW

- When we <u>prepare</u>, we get something ready for an activity.
- We <u>prepare</u> when we get ready to do something that we expect will happen.
- When we <u>prepare</u>, we gather things needed for an activity.
- We can <u>prepare</u> by planning details.
- We <u>prepare</u> by making something ready to use.

🗩 COLLABORATE

When we look back at what this word means, we see that it means to get ready to do something or to gather things needed for an activity.

① Brainstorm with a classmate a place you would like to see that would require an airline flight.

② Discuss how you would <u>prepare</u> for the flight.

③ Work together to create your own "pre-flight" checklist of what you would need to bring and do to <u>prepare</u> for your journey. Use a separate piece of paper.

④ As time allows, share your checklist with another pair of students to get their feedback on how well you <u>prepared</u>.

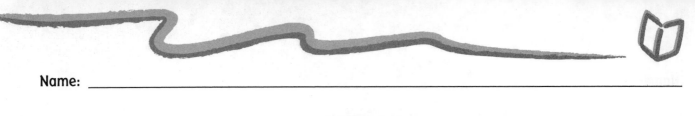

Name: _____

ARGUE

DEFINE

Question: What does it mean to <u>argue</u>?
Answer: When we <u>argue</u>, we give our opinion about something. We might give reasons or other evidence for or against a stated opinion.

STUDY

Sample Prompt: What would you <u>argue</u> natural gas companies should do to protect the environment?
Sample Answer: To conserve water, natural gas companies should try to reuse water in gas-production processes. They should carefully manage the transmission of chemical fluids, used to reduce the likelihood of potential leaks, that might pollute the environment.

Sample Prompt: What reason(s) can you give to <u>argue</u> against the United States importing liquefied natural gas?
Sample Answer: This form of natural gas requires processing before and after shipment, which adds to its overall cost and energy use. There is also the cost of shipping the natural gas to its end user.

PRACTICE

① **Task:** Read print and online materials about natural methane gas.

② **Prompt:** What reasons would you give to argue in favor of methane gas production?

_____

_____

_____

_____

_____

③ **Prompt:** What reasons would you give to argue against methane gas production?

_____

_____

_____

_____

_____

ARGUE (cont.)

☑ CHECK

Look back at what the word argue means.

① In a small group, read and discuss the paragraph below. Then answer the questions using a separate piece of paper.

Natural gas is a fossil fuel that produces less carbon dioxide than coal or oil. New technology has made it more cost effective to extract shale gas, a form of natural gas found in shale rocks. Some geologists estimate the United States has enough shale resources to last for the next one hundred years. Not everyone feels the benefits of shale gas production are worth it, however. The drilling process requires large amounts of water. This reduces the availability of water for other uses. Another concern is that chemicals used in the process will contaminate drinking-water supplies and natural habitats. Natural gas is a clean-burning fuel, and the large amounts available make this natural resource a valid option to pursue.

② What evidence does the author present to argue for his or her opinion?

③ What evidence does the author use to argue against others' opinions on this issue?

④ Discuss the paragraph and questions with your group. Argue for your opinion, using reasons and evidence from the passage as well as any knowledge you have of the topic.

⑤ Work together to write a statement to argue for a group opinion.

⑥ Share your opinion statement with other classmates.

🔍 REVIEW

- When we argue a point, we give reasons for or against it.
- We can give evidence when we argue for our opinion.
- When we argue, we try to prove we are right by giving reasons.
- We can argue by writing ideas in order to change someone's opinion about what is true or what should be done.

💬 COLLABORATE

When we look back at what this word means, we see that it means to give reasons for or against a stated opinion.

① Read a classmate's responses to Practice Prompts #2 and #3.

② Do you agree or disagree with your partner's responses? Write a reply to argue if his or her reasons and evidence make sense. Use a separate piece of paper.

INDICATE

DEFINE

Question: What does it mean to <u>indicate</u> something?
Answer: When we <u>indicate</u> something, we show it. We <u>indicate</u> something by pointing it out clearly or by directing attention to it. We can <u>indicate</u> something to show a need for it or to show that it is true.

STUDY

Sample Prompt: <u>Indicate</u> which part of a plant helps provide nourishment so the plant can grow.
Sample Answer: The roots absorb water and other nutrients from the soil and also store nutrients for the plant.

Sample Prompt: What is one characteristic of a tree that <u>indicates</u> its history?
Sample Answer: Scientists can study tree rings, which <u>indicate</u> the tree's health and growth over time.

✏ PRACTICE

① **Prompt:** What kinds of words and phrases could you use to <u>indicate</u> the types of experiences people have with plants?

_____

_____

_____

_____

② **Prompt:** Write a story about a character's experience with an unusual plant. Be sure to <u>indicate</u> the setting and situation, as well as the character's interactions with the plant. Think about what the word <u>indicate</u> means as you develop your narrative. Write your story on a separate piece of paper.

③ **Task:** Circle words in Practice Prompt #2 that <u>indicate</u> what you are supposed to do when you respond to the prompt.

④ **Prompt:** What will your character do and say to <u>indicate</u> his or her reactions and feelings about the experience with a plant?

_____

_____

_____

_____

INDICATE (cont.)

☑ CHECK

Look back at what the word <u>indicate</u> means.

Use a separate piece of paper to complete these activities:

① Work with a small group to study one or more plants and take notes to <u>indicate</u> your findings. 🖊️

② What examples can you find that <u>indicate</u> the best way to study a plant?

③ <u>Indicate</u> the plant your group chose to study and the steps you will take to study it. <u>Indicate</u> the resources you will use for your investigation.

④ How will you <u>indicate</u> which part of the plant changes nutrients into food?

⑤ What are some other ways you could <u>indicate</u> the same information?

⑥ How could you <u>indicate</u> one or more common uses of this plant?

⑦ How might scientists <u>indicate</u> a need for further study of this plant?

🔍 REVIEW

- When we point to something to <u>indicate</u> it, we direct attention to it.
- When we <u>indicate</u> something, we show that it exists or is true.
- When we <u>indicate</u> something, we might show a need for it.
- We can <u>indicate</u> something by stating it clearly.

💬 COLLABORATE

When we look back at what this word means, we see that it means to point something out clearly.

① Read the story a classmate wrote for Practice Prompt #2.

② Trade this page with your partner's. Highlight words and phrases in the rubric below that <u>indicate</u> things your partner did well in his or her writing.

③ Use a different color to underline words and phrases to <u>indicate</u> areas your partner may want to continue to improve in his or her writing.

The narrative introduces one or more characters and establishes a setting and situation to orient readers.
The narrator describes events in the experience in an order that makes sense.
The author uses dialogue and description to describe the experience and to <u>indicate</u> how characters respond to events.
The author includes concrete words and sensory details to describe events in the narrative.
The narrative has a conclusion that flows naturally from the narrated experience and <u>indicates</u> a sense of closure.

Name: _____

COMPARE

 DEFINE

Question: What does it mean to <u>compare</u> two things or ideas?
Answer: When we <u>compare</u> two things or ideas, we judge them against each other. We look for how they are similar and different. If we know two things are similar, we might <u>compare</u> them to show how they are alike. Sometimes we <u>compare</u> two things to decide which is better based on certain qualities.

 STUDY

Sample Prompt: <u>Compare</u> two varieties of apples, and describe what you like about each.
Sample Answer: I like to eat Fuji apples because they are crunchy and juicy. Gravenstein apples are not as sweet, but they make tasty applesauce or baked apples with cinnamon and nutmeg.

Sample Prompt: <u>Compare</u> the ways you and someone in your family eat a particular fruit.
Sample Answer: My mom likes sliced peaches, peach cobbler, and peach jam. I mostly eat sliced peaches because I think fresh peaches taste better than cooked peaches.

✎ **PRACTICE**

① **Prompt:** Write a journal entry to <u>compare</u> a fruit you like to eat in the summer with a fruit you like to eat in the winter.

_____

_____

_____

_____

② **Prompt:** How are the characteristics of these fruits similar? How are they different?

_____

_____

_____

③ **Prompt:** Which of the two fruits do you prefer? Why? In your opinion, which qualities make this fruit better?

_____

_____

_____

COMPARE *(cont.)*

☑ CHECK

Look back at what the word <u>compare</u> means.

① Work with a small group to <u>compare</u> fruit grown in different parts of the country. Indicate the region where you live. Choose a different area of the country to <u>compare</u> with your area.

② Choose one or more specific fruits to <u>compare</u>. Discuss these questions with your group:

- How would you <u>compare</u> fruit grown in your part of the country with fruit grown in another part of the country?
- What characteristics will you use to <u>compare</u> fruit grown in these two areas? Consider factors such as growing season, climate, soil conditions, etc.

③ Research to <u>compare</u> the fruit(s) grown in each area.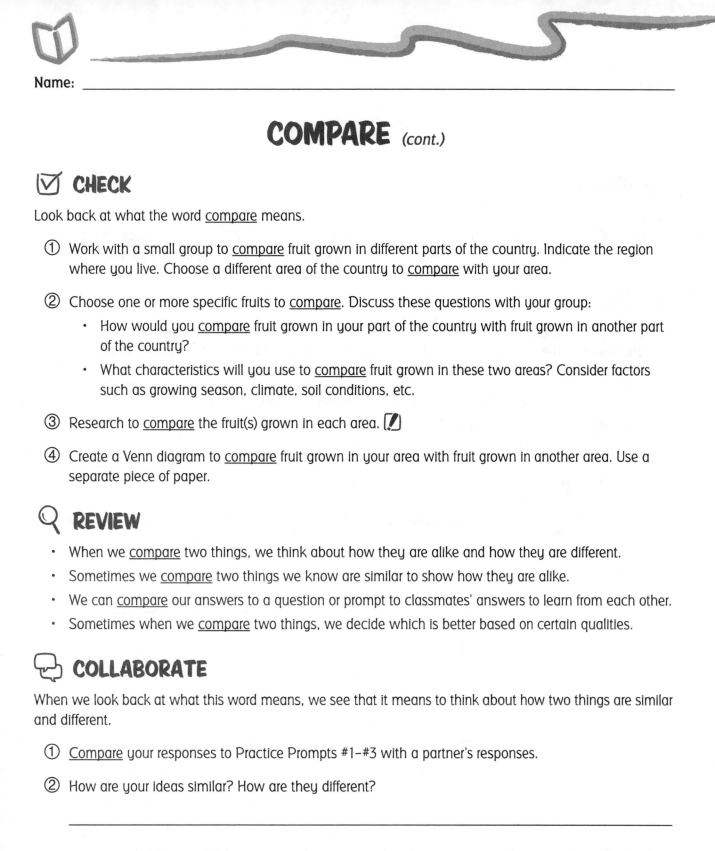

④ Create a Venn diagram to <u>compare</u> fruit grown in your area with fruit grown in another area. Use a separate piece of paper.

🔍 REVIEW

- When we <u>compare</u> two things, we think about how they are alike and how they are different.
- Sometimes we <u>compare</u> two things we know are similar to show how they are alike.
- We can <u>compare</u> our answers to a question or prompt to classmates' answers to learn from each other.
- Sometimes when we <u>compare</u> two things, we decide which is better based on certain qualities.

💬 COLLABORATE

When we look back at what this word means, we see that it means to think about how two things are similar and different.

① <u>Compare</u> your responses to Practice Prompts #1–#3 with a partner's responses.

② How are your ideas similar? How are they different?

_____

_____

_____

_____

_____

③ Discuss with your partner what you learned by <u>comparing</u> your responses.

Name: _____

CONTRAST

 DEFINE

Question: What does it mean to <u>contrast</u> two things or ideas?
Answer: When we <u>contrast</u> two things or ideas, we name how they are different. We look closely to see the differences when we <u>contrast</u> two things. We might <u>contrast</u> more than two things in a group.

 STUDY

Sample Prompt: <u>Contrast</u> the duration of the Great Depression and the Great Recession.
Sample Answer: The Great Depression lasted ten years, from 1929 to 1939. The Great Recession lasted less than two years, from December of 2007 to June of 2009.

Sample Prompt: Why do we learn and practice <u>contrasting</u> two or more things?
Sample Answer: Learning to <u>contrast</u> helps us develop critical-thinking skills that we use in classroom learning and everyday life.

✎ **PRACTICE**

① **Task:** Use appropriate print and online resources to research the Great Depression and the Great Recession. 🖊

② **Prompt:** How would you <u>contrast</u> the Great Depression and the Great Recession?

_____

_____

_____

③ **Prompt:** <u>Contrast</u> how each economic downturn affected people and the way they lived.

_____

_____

_____

④ **Prompt:** Compare and <u>contrast</u> the structure of two or more sources you read in your research. How is each text organized (chronology, comparison, cause and effect, problem and solution, etc.)?

_____

_____

_____

CONTRAST *(cont.)*

☑ CHECK

Look back at what the word <u>contrast</u> means.

① Your teacher will suggest print and digital fiction stories about the Great Depression that can be accessed from various library sources. 📝

② With a small literature group, read a few pages or a chapter of a story about the Great Depression.

Use a separate piece of paper to complete these activities:

③ Compare and <u>contrast</u> two or more characters, settings, or events in the story. Note your findings in a Venn diagram.

④ Meet with another group to compare and <u>contrast</u> the story you read with the story they read. How does each story approach the topic? <u>Contrast</u> the theme of each story.

⑤ Compare and <u>contrast</u> how characters speak in each story. What differences in language use do you notice?

🔍 REVIEW

- We <u>contrast</u> two things when we look closely to see how they are different.
- When we <u>contrast</u> two things, we point out and show how they are different.
- Sometimes, we <u>contrast</u> more than two things in a group.
- Often, when we <u>contrast</u> two things, we also compare them to see how they are alike.

💬 COLLABORATE

When we look back at what this word means, we see that it means to think about how two things are different.

① Review with a classmate what you have learned in your research about strengths and weaknesses of the economy.

② <u>Contrast</u> the characteristics of a strong economy and a weak economy.

_____

_____

③ <u>Contrast</u> the factors that contribute to an economic "boom" or a depression.

_____

_____

④ Work together to create a graphic organizer to demonstrate your understanding of the topic. Based on your learning, include at least one idea for how you could contribute to a strong economy through your family, school, or local community. Use a separate piece of paper.

APPLY

DEFINE

Question: What does it mean to <u>apply</u>?
Answer: When we <u>apply</u>, we put something to use for a practical purpose. We <u>apply</u> something when we bring it into action.

STUDY

Sample Prompt: How do scientists <u>apply</u> satellite imaging in different situations?
Sample Answer: Satellite imaging from the International Space Station (ISS) helps scientists track and understand natural disasters, such as floods or volcanic eruptions.

Sample Prompt: What is one technology from the ISS that has been <u>applied</u> to situations on Earth?
Sample Answer: Astronauts developed an air-purification system to help them grow plants for food in space. This technology is <u>applied</u> to keep fruits and vegetables fresh longer in grocery stores.

PRACTICE

① **Task:** Read the passage below about technology from the ISS.

One of the primary goals of the ISS is to conduct research. Those living aboard the station need clean drinking water. The technology used to purify water for those aboard the station can also be used in at-risk areas on Earth. The remote aspect of medical care for astronauts can be applied to bring medical services to people who live in remote areas on Earth. Astronauts live in a low-gravity environment aboard the space station. This leads to loss of bone and muscle. Astronauts experiment with exercise and vitamins to improve their health. Their findings will also help people on Earth. The technology that results from research and experiments on the ISS benefits astronauts and people living on Earth.

② **Task:** On a separate piece of paper, answer the guided questions below to <u>apply</u> information and evidence from the text.

- What is the author's purpose in the text?
- How well did he or she achieve that purpose?
- What might be the pros and cons to the experiments astronauts do to prevent bone and muscle loss?
- How do scientists <u>apply</u> remote technology used on the space station to situations on Earth?
- In your opinion, which technology developed on the ISS is most important to <u>apply</u> to improve life on Earth? Why?

Name: _____

APPLY *(cont.)*

☑ CHECK

Look back at what the word <u>apply</u> means.

① <u>Apply</u> what you already know about space-station technology to write questions to learn more about the topic.

_____

_____

② Research with classmates to learn more about technology on the ISS.

③ Discuss with classmates how we <u>apply</u> technology from the ISS and other space explorations to our everyday lives.

④ What could you do to <u>apply</u> what you learned from the class discussion about ISS technology to your life?

_____

_____

⚲ REVIEW

- When we <u>apply</u> something, we use it to have an effect.
- We can <u>apply</u> knowledge and learning by putting it into action.
- We <u>apply</u> something when we put it to use.

💬 COLLABORATE

When we look back at what this word means, we see that it means to put knowledge or learning to use for a practical purpose.

① Read print and online materials to learn more about space technology that we <u>apply</u> and use in our everyday lives.

② Choose one technology you have observed or have experienced.

③ Talk with a partner about how this technology was <u>applied</u> to solve a problem.

④ Discuss another technology you read about. How could you <u>apply</u> this technology to solve a current problem? Draw a diagram to show your ideas. Use a separate piece of paper.

⑤ In what other ways could you <u>apply</u> this information and knowledge?

_____

_____

EXPRESS

DEFINE

Question: What does it mean to <u>express</u> ourselves?

Answer: When we <u>express</u> ourselves, we show what we feel or think by saying, doing, or writing something. We can <u>express</u> an opinion, an idea, thoughts, or feelings.

STUDY

Sample Prompt: <u>Express</u> your opinion of skimboarding.

Sample Answer: Skimboarding is a fun, easy water sport for kids to do. The only equipment you need is a thin board. You don't always get wet, which is important if the water is cold.

Sample Prompt: How would you <u>express</u> your thoughts and feelings about snorkeling?

Sample Answer: I would write details about why I enjoy it. I could show someone a picture of me wearing a snorkel mask and grinning. I could tell a friend what it feels like to snorkel.

✎ PRACTICE

① **Task:** Choose an ocean sport about which you would like to write a real or imagined experience.

② **Task:** On a separate piece of paper, create a web to brainstorm descriptive words and sensory details that will best <u>express</u> the thoughts, feelings, and actions of the narrator in your story.

③ **Prompt:** Write sentences to describe what happens in the story. Imagine you are experiencing the events of the story yourself to better <u>express</u> what the narrator would say or do in the situation.

_____

_____

_____

_____

④ **Prompt:** What obstacles or conflict does the narrator experience? How will you <u>express</u> his or her response to those problems?

_____

_____

_____

_____

⑤ **Prompt:** On a separate piece of paper, write your story about an ocean sport. Use your notes from Practice Task #2 and Practice Prompts #3 and #4 to help you <u>express</u> your ideas clearly.

EXPRESS (cont.)

☑ CHECK

Look back at what the word <u>express</u> means.

① Talk with classmates in a small group about ocean kayaking. What have you heard or read about this sport? What would you like to learn about it? <u>Express</u> your ideas clearly in your small-group discussion.

② What ideas did others in the group <u>express</u>? How do their ideas compare with your thoughts about the topic?

_____

_____

_____

③ Write one thought that one of your classmates <u>expressed</u>.

_____

_____

🔍 REVIEW

- When we <u>express</u> something, we talk or write about it.
- We might <u>express</u> our opinion about something to other people by saying it or writing it.
- We can <u>express</u> an idea by showing it with a sign or a symbol.
- We can do something other than talking or writing to <u>express</u> our thoughts or feelings about something.

💬 COLLABORATE

When we look back at what this word means, we see that it means to show what we think or feel about something by talking, writing, or doing some action.

① Read a classmate's story that he or she wrote for Practice Prompt #5.

② How would you <u>express</u> the author's main idea in your own words?

_____

_____

③ <u>Express</u> your understanding of your partner's story to him or her. Show kindness and respect as you talk about your classmate's writing.

④ Work together with your partner to create symbols or simple drawings to <u>express</u> what happens in the story to accompany your writing.

Name: _____

CATEGORIZE

 DEFINE

Question: What does it mean to categorize?
Answer: When we categorize, we put things into groups based on characteristics they have in common. When we categorize, we organize things or information in a way that makes sense.

 STUDY

Sample Prompt: How would you categorize the types of climates in which nut trees grow?
Sample Answer: Some nut trees grow best in a temperate zone with a certain number of cold winter days. Other nut trees grow in tropical areas. A few nut trees like short, cold winters and hot, dry summers, so they do well in the American southwest.

Sample Prompt: Categorize nuts based on how people prepare nuts to eat.
Sample Answer: Many nuts have shells. People shell the nuts and then eat them raw. Sometimes nuts are roasted in oil or without oil. Nuts can be pressed to make oils or ground to make flour.

✎ **PRACTICE**

① **Task:** List the types of nuts your friends and family like to eat.

_____

_____

② **Prompt:** What characteristics do the nuts you listed in Practice Task #1 have?

_____

_____

③ **Prompt:** Based on their characteristics, how would you categorize the nuts you listed in Practice Task #1?

_____

_____

④ **Prompt:** Think about how you categorized nuts in Practice Prompt #3. Which group of nuts do you think you would most enjoy? Why?

_____

_____

CATEGORIZE (cont.)

☑ CHECK

Look back at what the word <u>categorize</u> means.

① Work together as a class to brainstorm ways you could <u>categorize</u> the topic of nuts.

② On an interactive whiteboard or chart paper, create a web to record the ideas you and your classmates discuss. 🖉

③ Study the class-generated web and then write a sample writing prompt for the topic.

_____

_____

④ As time allows, share your writing prompt with classmates in a small group.

⑤ Discuss: How did <u>categorizing</u> ideas help you better understand the topic to prepare to write about it?

🔍 REVIEW

- When we <u>categorize</u>, we put people or things into a group with similar characteristics.
- We organize things when we <u>categorize</u> them.

💬 COLLABORATE

When we look back at what this word means, we see that it means to put things into groups based on similar characteristics.

Use a separate piece of paper to complete these activities:

① Study the paragraph below. Discuss with a partner how you would <u>categorize</u> nuts based on the information you read.

Growers plant nut-bearing trees in orchards. The type of nut trees planted in an orchard depends on the climate. Different varieties require different amounts of space. Growers know how many trees they can plant on an acre of land for best nut production. Another factor to consider is how many years it takes for trees to begin producing nuts. People who plant orchards research the best variety of nut tree for their area.

② Which key words in the passage help you determine appropriate categories?

③ What similarities and differences in the key words do you notice? How could you group these key words into similar categories?

④ Work together to create a chart you could use to <u>categorize</u> nuts. Who might be most interested in reading your chart? How would the information help your audience?

Name: _____

PREDICT

 DEFINE

Question: What does it mean to <u>predict</u>?
Answer: When we <u>predict</u>, we say what we think will happen in the future. We use our experience or look at what we have seen to <u>predict</u> what we think will happen next.

 STUDY

Sample Prompt: How do our own experiences help us <u>predict</u> what might happen next in a story?
Sample Answer: We can think about how we have solved similar problems or what we might do next in a similar situation.

Sample Prompt: How might the time of year or weather help readers <u>predict</u> what happens next in a story?
Sample Answer: Readers can think about what the weather is like at different times of the year. Then they can <u>predict</u> what characters might do in certain types of weather.

 PRACTICE

① **Task:** Read the story excerpt below. Use a separate piece of paper to respond to the writing prompts.

Alexa turned around so Josiah could make sure her water bottle was cinched into the outer pocket of her backpack. "Ready?" he asked. She nodded and followed him onto the rocky trail. Shaded from the sun, it felt almost cool. Within a quarter mile, though, they started to ascend the first ridge. Alexa wiped her forehead, already looking forward to their first rest point, even though she wouldn't dare drink much water. They would need all the water they carried on the eight-mile hike in and out of the jungle.

② **Prompt:** Which words in the story give clues you can use to <u>predict</u> what will happen next?

③ **Prompt:** What dialogue or character actions help you <u>predict</u> what will happen next?

④ **Prompt:** What do you <u>predict</u> will happen next in the story?

⑤ **Prompt:** What do you <u>predict</u> the outcome would be if one of the characters lost a water bottle in the jungle?

PREDICT *(cont.)*

☑ CHECK

Look back at what the word <u>predict</u> means.

① Work with classmates in a small group to discuss your experience with <u>predicting</u> what will happen next in a situation.

② Think of an outdoor adventure you or your classmates have had, perhaps together as a class. Discuss your answers to these questions:
  - What happened during that experience?
  - How did each event that happened help you <u>predict</u> and prepare for what might happen next?

⚲ REVIEW

  - We <u>predict</u> something when we tell what we think will happen in the future.
  - When we <u>predict</u>, we look at what we have seen to say what we think will happen next.
  - We can use our experience and what we know to help us <u>predict</u> what will happen next.

💬 COLLABORATE

When we look back at what this word means, we see that it means to say what we think will happen in the future.

① Read the story starter below.

One day when Taylor and I were out roaming in the woods, we heard a horse coming just before we got to the trail.

② What do you <u>predict</u> will happen next?

_____

_____

_____

_____

③ Refer to your response to #2 to write the next paragraph in the story. Use a separate piece of paper.

④ Trade your paragraph with a partner.

⑤ How closely does your partner's paragraph match what you <u>predicted</u> would happen in the story? Discuss your ideas with each other and why you <u>predicted</u> the next part of the story the way you did.

Name: _____

CONCLUDE/DRAW A CONCLUSION

DEFINE

Question: What does it mean to <u>conclude</u> something? How do we <u>draw a conclusion</u>?

Answer: When we <u>conclude</u> something, we finish it. We can <u>conclude</u> a piece of writing by restating the topic in different words. When we <u>draw a conclusion</u>, we use facts or reasons to make a decision. We might realize something based on those facts.

STUDY

Sample Task: Read the sentence below. <u>Draw a conclusion</u> based on what you read.

Some metropolitan areas have "L trains," which run on elevated tracks or underground as subways.

Sample Answer: Rail-based mass transit runs wherever space is available in a crowded city.

Sample Prompt: What facts or reasons might lead someone to <u>draw the conclusion</u> below?

The history of Boston's transit system provides important clues to its future.

Sample Answer: Someone might have read facts about the original construction of Boston's subway line and how weather affects the system. A writer might then list reasons for improvements and future projects. The sentence above might <u>conclude</u> such a paragraph.

PRACTICE

Use a separate piece of paper to complete these activities:

① **Prompt:** Write a question or opinion you have about high-speed rail.

② **Task:** Research high-speed rail, using your response to Practice Prompt #1 as a focus for your research. Take notes on your findings, including sources. [✎]

③ **Prompt:** Plan a paragraph about high-speed rail based on what you have learned. What impression do you want to leave with readers as you <u>conclude</u> your paragraph?

④ **Prompt:** How will you <u>draw a conclusion</u> that follows from the information you will present in your paragraph?

⑤ **Prompt:** Use your research notes to write a paragraph about high-speed rail.

⑥ **Prompt:** How did you state your main idea in a different way to <u>conclude</u> your paragraph?

CONCLUDE/DRAW A CONCLUSION (cont.)

☑ CHECK

Look back at what the word conclude means. Think about what it means to conclude something or to draw a conclusion.

Use a separate piece of paper to complete these activities:

① Work with a small group to research light rail, subways, and other forms of rail-based mass transit. 📄

② Draw conclusions about the topic based on what you read, and take notes about what you conclude.

③ What do you and your classmates conclude about mass transit in your area? If you do not live in a metropolitan area, think of another city in your state. Is mass transit available? If so, how effective is it in serving public transportation needs? If not, which form of rail-based mass transit might be feasible or beneficial?

④ Find another small group with different opinions and debate what you conclude about rail-based mass transit. Support your ideas and opinions with facts and details from your research.

🔍 REVIEW

- When we conclude something, we bring it to an end. We finish it.
- We draw a conclusion when we decide something using reasons.
- We can conclude something based on facts.
- We can conclude something by restating the topic in different words.

💬 COLLABORATE

When we look back at what conclude and draw a conclusion mean, we see that they mean to use facts and reasons to decide something or provide a final sentence.

① Read the paragraph below with a partner. Then answer the questions that follow on a separate piece of paper.

Cities have different forms of mass transit to help many people get from one place to another. Some forms of mass transit use railways. Overhead electrical wires power trains that run on tracks. Often, the tracks are separate from street traffic. Light rail makes frequent stops, and routes run within a metropolitan area. Commuter rail is another form of rail-based mass transit. Diesel-electric locomotives pull trains on existing railroads that are also used by freight trains. Commuter rail has fewer station stops, and a route might be as long as fifty miles.

② How would you conclude this paragraph? Write one or two sentences and then share your sentences with your partner.

③ What facts and reasons did your partner use to draw a conclusion?

④ How did you and your partner each restate the topic in different words to conclude the paragraph?

Name: _____

RECOMMEND

DEFINE

Question: What does it mean to <u>recommend</u>?

Answer: When we <u>recommend</u>, we suggest that something or someone is good or worthy. We might suggest that someone do something in particular.

STUDY

Sample Prompt: Which movie would you <u>recommend</u> to a friend?

Sample Answer: I would <u>recommend</u> *Mary Poppins* because it has funny characters.

Sample Prompt: Which sources do you most trust to <u>recommend</u> a movie you might like to watch?

Sample Answer: I would trust my family and friends to <u>recommend</u> a movie I would like because they know me. They spend time with me and understand the kinds of things I like and don't like.

✎ PRACTICE

① **Prompt:** Why is it important to watch a movie before you <u>recommend</u> it to someone else?

_____

_____

_____

② **Prompt:** Would you <u>recommend</u> kids always watch a movie with a grown-up present? Why or why not?

_____

_____

_____

③ **Prompt:** Which movie would you <u>recommend</u> as a good family movie? Why?

_____

_____

_____

④ **Prompt:** Which movie would you <u>recommend</u> be shown in your class on a movie day? Why?

_____

_____

_____

RECOMMEND (cont.)

☑ CHECK

Look back at what the word <u>recommend</u> means.

① Work together with classmates to discuss criteria you would use to <u>recommend</u> a movie.

② Create a list of criteria you could use to <u>recommend</u> a movie to someone.

_____

_____

③ Why is it helpful to refer to such a list to <u>recommend</u> a movie for someone to watch?

_____

_____

④ What is the most important factor from your list to consider when <u>recommending</u> a movie? Why?

_____

_____

🔍 REVIEW

- When we <u>recommend</u> something, we say it is good and worthy of being chosen.
- We can <u>recommend</u> or suggest that someone do something in particular.

💬 COLLABORATE

When we look back at what this word means, we see that it means to suggest something as being good and worthy of being chosen.

① Write a letter to a classmate to <u>recommend</u> a movie he or she might like to watch. Include at least two reasons why you would <u>recommend</u> this movie. Use a separate piece of paper.

② Exchange letters with a classmate.

③ Ask your partner questions about the movie he or she <u>recommended</u> to you.

④ Do you think you would like the movie your partner <u>recommended</u>? Why or why not?

_____

_____

_____

DEFEND

DEFINE

Question: What does it mean to <u>defend</u> something?

Answer: When we <u>defend</u> something, we support our ideas with an argument that includes facts and reasons. We <u>defend</u> something by writing or speaking to support it. When we <u>defend</u> something, we fight to keep it.

STUDY

Sample Prompt: How might we <u>defend</u> the freedom granted in the Emancipation Proclamation issued by President Lincoln?

Sample Answer: The proclamation freed all slaves in the United States. We can <u>defend</u> that freedom by remembering the original documents stating that all men are equal. We can <u>defend</u> this freedom with our actions by treating everyone fairly.

Sample Prompt: The United States Citizenship Resource Center lists supporting and <u>defending</u> the Constitution as a responsibility of citizens. How might a citizen fulfill this responsibility?

Sample Answer: A citizen could <u>defend</u> the Constitution by speaking respectfully about our Constitution and voting for public officials who will follow the Constitution. A citizen could also explain to other people why the Constitution is an important part of living in America.

PRACTICE

① **Prompt:** What does it mean to <u>defend</u> as described in this quotation?

"Freedom is the sure possession of those alone who have the courage to <u>defend</u> it."
~ Pericles

_____

_____

_____

_____

② **Task:** Read the first few lines of the Declaration of Independence printed below. Answer the questions that follow on a separate piece of paper.

"We hold these truths to be self-evident, that all men are created equal, that they are endowed by their Creator with certain unalienable Rights, that among these are Life, Liberty and the pursuit of Happiness."

③ **Prompt:** What rights or freedoms does the Declaration of Independence grant United States citizens?

④ **Task:** Review additional text from the Declaration of Independence as available. What details or evidence from the text could you use to <u>defend</u> your answer for Practice Prompt #3? ✏️

DEFEND *(cont.)*

☑ CHECK

Look back at what the word <u>defend</u> means.

① Work with a small group to review the Bill of Rights. 🖊

② Select one right to <u>defend</u> as a group.

③ Discuss how you will <u>defend</u> your ideas.

④ Work together to write a statement to <u>defend</u> that right. Include reasons why it is important for citizens to have this right. Use a separate piece of paper.

⑤ Present your statement to the class.

🔍 REVIEW

- We <u>defend</u> something when we support it with a logical argument.
- We can <u>defend</u> something by answering questions about it.
- We <u>defend</u> something when we fight or argue to keep it.

💬 COLLABORATE

When we look back at what this word means, we see that it means to use facts and reasons to support our ideas about a topic.

① With a partner, discuss why the right to vote is important. Discuss which groups of people should have the right to vote.

② How would you <u>defend</u> the right to vote? Complete the chart below to gather and record evidence to <u>defend</u> your position.

Facts	Reasons
Experiences	**Expert Opinions**

Name: _____

INVESTIGATE

 ## DEFINE

Question: What does it mean to <u>investigate</u>?
Answer: When we <u>investigate</u>, we find out as much as possible by observing or studying something closely.

 ## STUDY

Sample Prompt: What forms of transportation might someone <u>investigate</u> to travel around a city?
Sample Answer: A person could <u>investigate</u> cars, buses, and bicycles to get around in a city.

Sample Prompt: What is one question you will answer when you <u>investigate</u> buses as a form of transportation?
Sample Answer: I would <u>investigate</u> the cost of taking the bus and compare it to other forms of transportation.

PRACTICE

① **Prompt:** How could you <u>investigate</u> different forms of transportation?

_____

_____

_____

② **Task:** <u>Investigate</u> forms of transportation people pay a fee to use. 🖊

③ **Task:** Select one specific form of transportation you <u>investigated</u> in Practice Task #2 as a topic for an informative essay.

④ **Prompt:** Who might be most interested in the information you learned when you <u>investigated</u> this topic?

_____

⑤ **Prompt:** What key facts and information did you learn when you <u>investigated</u> this type of transportation?

_____

_____

_____

_____

⑥ **Prompt:** On a separate piece of paper, write an informative essay about the form of transportation you selected in Practice Task #3. Use your notes from Practice Task #2 and Practice Prompt #5 to plan your essay. <u>Investigate</u> your specific topic further as needed. Keep the audience you identified in Practice Prompt #4 in mind as you plan and write your essay.

INVESTIGATE (cont.)

☑ CHECK

Look back at what the word <u>investigate</u> means.

① As a class, brainstorm companies that provide rides for hire.

② <u>Investigate</u> what you and your classmates already know about this type of transportation.

③ On a separate piece of paper, create a chart with four rows and two columns. Label the first row of the first column "My Ideas." Label the first row of the second column "My Classmates' Ideas."

④ In the second row of the first column, write a fact or something you know about rides for hire. Share your fact or information with a classmate. Write the information you receive from your classmate in the second row of the second column.

⑤ Write another fact or detail in the third row of the first column. Share this information with a different classmate. Write the new information you receive from your classmate in the third row of the second column.

⑥ Go through the writing and sharing process with one more classmate to complete the chart.

⑦ How did sharing ideas with classmates help you <u>investigate</u> this form of transportation? Discuss your answer with your classmates.

🔍 REVIEW

· When we <u>investigate</u> something, we observe or study it closely.

· We <u>investigate</u> something by finding out facts about it.

· We try to get information about something when we <u>investigate</u> it.

💬 COLLABORATE

When we look back at what this word means, we see that it means to observe or study something closely to find out more about it.

① Work with a partner to discuss the questions listed below to <u>investigate</u> bicycles as a form of transportation. Take notes on a separate piece of paper.

    1. What have you observed about bicycles?

    2. What other forms of transportation would you compare bicycles to?

    3. Which is the most logical way to organize the thoughts and information you know about bicycles?

    4. What questions do you have about your partner's ideas?

    5. What inferences can you make from your discussion?

② Write a few sentences to explain what you learned about bicycles and why they might be a valid form of transportation for specific groups of people. Use the same separate piece of paper.

Name: _____

CITE

 DEFINE

Question: What does it mean to <u>cite</u> something?
Answer: When we <u>cite</u> something, we quote from a written work. We might <u>cite</u> something as an example. We can also <u>cite</u> something to support our opinion or ideas or as proof in an argument.

 STUDY

Sample Prompt: What is an important thing to remember when we <u>cite</u> from a written work?
Sample Answer: It is important to check that we <u>cited</u> accurately and have written the words correctly with correct punctuation.

Sample Prompt: Which historical documents might fifth-graders <u>cite</u> in their study of American history?
Sample Answer: Important historical documents students might <u>cite</u> include speeches. Two examples are Patrick Henry's "Give Me Liberty" speech and Martin Luther King's "I Have a Dream" speech.

✏️ **PRACTICE**

① **Task:** Read Lincoln's Gettysburg Address. 🔲

② **Prompt:** What was the purpose of the occasion when Lincoln gave this address?

_____

③ **Prompt:** <u>Cite</u> an example from the text that explains why people had gathered that day.

_____

_____

④ **Prompt:** What does Lincoln call on his audience to do?

_____

_____

⑤ **Prompt:** <u>Cite</u> evidence from the text to support your answer to Practice Prompt #4.

_____

_____

_____

_____

CITE *(cont.)*

☑ CHECK

Look back at what the word <u>cite</u> means.

① <u>Cite</u> an interesting fact, detail, or quote from a historical document you have reviewed. Post it on an interactive whiteboard or write it on an index card and post the card on a class bulletin board. 📝

② Read facts, details, or quotes <u>cited</u> by classmates.

③ Post responses to two or three of your classmates' posts. You might give an opinion about what a classmate <u>cited</u>. Or you might explain how the citation is an example of something.

④ Read any responses you received to the fact, detail, or quote you <u>cited</u>.

⑤ As a class, discuss the quotes you <u>cited</u> and your responses to continue the conversation.

🔍 REVIEW

· When we <u>cite</u>, we say the words from a book or other written work.
· When we <u>cite</u> something, we say it as an example to support an idea or an opinion.
· When we <u>cite</u> something, we might use it as proof of an argument.
· We can <u>cite</u> something to call attention to it as an example.

💬 COLLABORATE

When we look back at what this word means, we see that it means to quote from a written work, particularly as an example to support an idea or opinion.

① Read a classmate's responses to Practice Prompts #4 and #5.

② How well does the evidence your partner <u>cited</u> support his or her answer to Practice Prompt #4? Share your answer with your partner.

③ <u>Cite</u> the phrase or sentence from the Gettysburg Address that you find most meaningful and important for people today to remember.

_____

_____

_____

_____

④ Discuss your response to #3 above with your partner. Why did you <u>cite</u> that particular part of the speech?

Name: _____

QUESTION

 ## DEFINE

Question: What does it mean to question?

Answer: When we question, we ask for information from someone. We question to get information or to examine something. Other reasons we question are to test someone's knowledge about something or to express doubt about something.

 ## STUDY

Sample Prompt: Why did Ariana question what she heard about alligators?
Sample Answer: Ariana wasn't sure if alligators were still an endangered species.

Sample Prompt: Who could you question to learn more about endangered species?
Sample Answer: I could question a teacher, librarian, or expert to learn more about endangered species.

PRACTICE

① **Task:** Read the paragraph below about soft-shelled turtles.

Some turtles have soft shells. One species in particular, the Yangtze giant softshell turtle, lives in Asia. Only three of these turtles exist in the world today, making them critically endangered. These amazing turtles can live up to one hundred years and weigh nearly two hundred pounds. Development along their freshwater habitat devastated natural populations of the turtles.

② **Prompt:** What is one thing you question about what you read?

_____

_____

_____

_____

_____

_____

③ **Task:** Underline a phrase or sentence in the paragraph about which you question the meaning.

④ **Prompt:** Who could you question to learn more about what the paragraph means?

_____

_____

_____

Name: _____

QUESTION *(cont.)*

☑ CHECK

Look back at what the word <u>question</u> means.

① Complete the Q-A-R chart below to <u>question</u> and learn about why species become endangered.

Question	Ask	Responses

② Think about what you already know about the circumstances that lead to endangered species. What is one idea you <u>question</u>? Write your thoughts in the first column of the chart.

③ In the second column of the chart, write sentences to ask classmates about why species become endangered.

④ <u>Question</u> your classmates to learn what they think and know about the topic.

⑤ In the third column of the chart, record classmates' responses when you <u>questioned</u> them.

ℚ REVIEW

- We <u>question</u> to ask someone for information about something.
- We <u>question</u> to examine something.
- We might <u>question</u> to express doubt about something.
- We can <u>question</u> to test someone's knowledge about something.

🗩 COLLABORATE

When we look back at this word, we see that it means to ask someone about something.

① Why might people <u>question</u> the need to protect endangered species?

② Work with a partner to consider both sides of the issue.

③ Create a Venn diagram to <u>question</u> and explore the positions people might take about protecting endangered species. Use a separate piece of paper.

ASSESS

DEFINE

Question: What does it mean to <u>assess</u>?
Answer: When we <u>assess</u>, we judge how good or bad something is. We determine the importance or value of something.

STUDY

Sample Prompt: How would you <u>assess</u> the importance of neighborhood parks in a city?
Sample Answer: It is important to have neighborhood parks throughout the city and at different locations. This makes it easier for people to enjoy the benefits of parks, and more people will use the parks.

Sample Prompt: <u>Assess</u> the value of a tree canopy in a community.
Sample Answer: Tree canopies make communities better places in which to live by lowering summer temperatures and providing cleaner air quality.

✎ PRACTICE

① **Prompt:** How would you <u>assess</u> the value of urban forests in metropolitan areas?

_____

_____

_____

_____

② **Prompt:** What factors or criteria did you use to <u>assess</u> urban forests in Practice Prompt #1?

_____

_____

_____

_____

③ **Prompt:** Why is it important to <u>assess</u> the role of urban forests, as well as the role of other urban features, in cities?

_____

_____

_____

_____

ASSESS *(cont.)*

☑ CHECK

Look back at what the word <u>assess</u> means.

① Work with a small group to <u>assess</u> the amount and quality of green space in your community.

Use separate pieces of paper to complete these activities:

② Sketch a general diagram of your community, including existing green spaces.

③ Work together to develop a plan to incorporate more green space in your community.

④ As a group, write a letter to one or more leaders in your community, describing the factors you considered when <u>assessing</u> the need for and/or quality of green space in your community. Attach your diagram and plan to the letter.

⌕ REVIEW

· We <u>assess</u> something when we determine how important or valuable it is.
· We judge how good or bad something is when we <u>assess</u> it.

💬 COLLABORATE

When we look back at what this word means, we see that it means to determine the value or importance of something.

① Read a classmate's response to Practice Prompt #1.

② How could you <u>assess</u> your partner's understanding of the topic?

_____

_____

_____

_____

_____

_____

_____

③ <u>Assess</u> how well your classmate communicated his or her ideas about urban forests. Write your comments on one or more sticky notes to mark specific places in your partner's writing. Remember to show kindness and respect in your comments.

Name: _____

ARRANGE

DEFINE

Question: What does it mean to _arrange_?
Answer: When we _arrange_, we place things in a specific order or position. We can _arrange_ plans or details for something to happen.

STUDY

Sample Prompt: What is the best way to _arrange_ a rock garden?
Sample Answer: _Arrange_ the plants and rocks so that the garden looks natural.

Sample Prompt: What do you need to _arrange_ an herb garden?
Sample Answer: When _arranging_ an herb garden, you need to have a good location. _Arrange_ to grow the herbs in the right amount of sunlight and in the right kind of soil.

PRACTICE

① **Prompt:** Write a paragraph to describe how you would _arrange_ a flower garden.

_____

_____

_____

_____

_____

_____

_____

_____

② **Prompt:** Suggest a different way to _arrange_ a flower garden.

_____

_____

③ **Prompt:** What would happen if you _arranged_ the flower garden in a different way than the way you described in Practice Prompt #1?

_____

_____

ARRANGE (cont.)

☑ CHECK

Look back at what the word <u>arrange</u> means.

① What factors are important to consider when you <u>arrange</u> a vegetable garden?

② As a class, list criteria on an interactive whiteboard or chart paper. 📝

③ Work with a small group to learn about a criterion listed. Why is this factor important in <u>arranging</u> a garden? How would you <u>arrange</u> a garden to reflect this factor?

_____

_____

_____

_____

④ Share your ideas with other classmates.

⑤ Combine your ideas to create a diagram showing how you would <u>arrange</u> a vegetable garden at your school. Use a separate piece of paper.

🔍 REVIEW

- When we <u>arrange</u> things, we move them into a certain order or position.
- We can <u>arrange</u> things by placing them in an interesting order.
- When we make plans for something to happen, we <u>arrange</u> for it to happen.
- When we <u>arrange</u> for something to happen, we plan the details before it happens.

💬 COLLABORATE

When we look back at what this word means, we see that it means to place things in an order that makes sense or to plan details of something that will happen.

① Discuss the following questions with a partner to <u>arrange</u> how you would plant a garden with friends.

- What tasks would need to be done?
- Who would be in charge of each task?
- What tools and supplies would you need?
- When would be the best time to plant the garden?

② Work together to write a plan describing how you would <u>arrange</u> planting the garden. Use a separate piece of paper.

Name: _____

ANALYZE

 DEFINE

Question: What does it mean to <u>analyze</u>?
Answer: When we <u>analyze</u>, we look at something carefully in order to understand it. We might think about information in a text or graphic feature. We <u>analyze</u> when we break text into parts to understand the relationship between ideas.

 STUDY

Sample Prompt: How might we <u>analyze</u> a character in a story?
Sample Answer: We could identify a character's attributes and how they affect events in the story.

Sample Prompt: What strategies can you use to <u>analyze</u> a passage?
Sample Answer: I can look for context clues to understand the meanings of words and phrases, identify similarities and differences between certain aspects of the passage, and write questions to think about the text in different ways.

 PRACTICE

① **Task:** Read the story excerpt below. Then respond to the prompts on a separate piece of paper.

Ella stretched her legs as straight as she could under the seat in front of her. "When is our next stop?" She tried to keep her voice calm even though she ached to get out of the car. Dad said they would stop in ten minutes or so at a marker on a national historic trail in Nebraska. Ella stared out the window at the endless prairie that looked deceptively flat. She perked up as they took the next exit off the interstate. After Dad parked the car, they wandered over to the marker. Mom read the sign aloud as Ella gazed at the dry, brown land before them. "Let's go! We can't see much from here." Ella set off impatiently toward the deep ruts in the prairie grass.

② **Prompt:** What is the story about? Which clues in this excerpt help you <u>analyze</u> the topic of the story?

③ **Prompt:** How would you <u>analyze</u> the author's purpose in writing this story?

④ **Prompt:** <u>Analyze</u> the setting in the story excerpt. What do you notice about the setting? How would you describe where this part of the story takes place?

⑤ **Prompt:** What are Ella's motives for her actions? How do they contribute to the overall plot?

⑥ **Prompt:** What visual or multimedia elements might contribute to readers' understanding of the story?

Name: _____

ANALYZE (cont.)

☑ CHECK

Look back at what the word <u>analyze</u> means.

  ① Your teacher will provide fiction or nonfiction texts about westward expansion. 🖊

Use a separate piece of paper to complete these activities:

  ② Work with a small group to read a sample passage and ask and answer questions to <u>analyze</u> what you read.

  ③ How would you describe the parts of the passage you will <u>analyze</u>? Is there an introduction or beginning? How does each sentence or part of the passage work with the other parts?

  ④ <u>Analyze</u> how each thought or idea in the passage leads to the next.

  ⑤ Read the passage more than once with your classmates to <u>analyze</u> and understand the author's message.

  ⑥ Write a sentence to state the main idea or theme of the passage.

🔍 REVIEW

- We <u>analyze</u> when we think about information in a text in different ways.
- One way to <u>analyze</u> a text is to break it into parts to understand the order or relationship of ideas.
- We use this skill of <u>analyzing</u> when we look at separate pieces of information presented in a chart.

💬 COLLABORATE

When we look back at what this word means, we see that it means to look at something carefully by breaking it into parts to understand more about it.

Use a separate piece of paper to complete these activities:

  ① With a partner, read another sample about westward expansion provided during the Check activity.

  ② Discuss with your partner the narrator's point of view in the sample you read with your small group in Check #2.

  ③ Identify the point of view in the sample passage you read with your partner in Collaborate #1.

  ④ How is each point of view similar or different?

  ⑤ <u>Analyze</u> other similarities and differences between the passage you read in the Check activity and the passage you read with your partner in this activity. Record your observations in a simple T-chart.

  ⑥ How does reading more than one passage about the same topic deepen your understanding of the subject?

EVALUATE

DEFINE

Question: What does it mean to _evaluate_?
Answer: When we _evaluate_, we think carefully about something to decide how good or valuable it is. We decide why something is important.

STUDY

Sample Prompt: Why is it important to _evaluate_ the food we eat away from home?
Sample Answer: When we _evaluate_ food we eat, we can use our insights to make choices in the future.

Sample Prompt: What strategies could you use to _evaluate_ information about food you would eat at a sporting event?
Sample Answer: I could use facts or personal experience or read other people's opinions to _evaluate_ stadium food.

PRACTICE

① **Prompt:** How would you _evaluate_ stadium food? What is your opinion of such food in general? (Some examples are hot dogs, nachos, and popcorn.) What facts or details did you _evaluate_ to arrive at your opinion?

_____

_____

② **Prompt:** _Evaluate_ the food choices people have at sports arenas. How healthy, affordable, or easy to eat are the choices offered at sporting events?

_____

_____

③ **Prompt:** How would you rate or _evaluate_ the quality of food offered at a local sports arena? Include reasons to support your response.

_____

_____

④ **Prompt:** Use a separate piece of paper to _evaluate_ the _Washington Post_ writer's opinion cited below. Based on your observations and experience, do you agree or disagree with the opinion? Include reasons to support your opinion.

"Gone are the days where concessions at sporting arenas would only offer hot dogs [and] popcorn." (_Washington Post_)

EVALUATE *(cont.)*

☑ CHECK

Look back at what the word <u>evaluate</u> means.

Use a separate piece of paper to complete these activities:

① Work with classmates in a small group to determine criteria you would use to <u>evaluate</u> stadium food. If you and your classmates do not have opportunities to visit stadiums, what criteria would you use to <u>evaluate</u> picnic food?

② Create a list of your criteria.

③ List one or more stadium or picnic foods you and others in your small group have tried.

④ Use your list of criteria to <u>evaluate</u> each food.

⑤ After you <u>evaluate</u> the foods, rate them to show which foods your group thinks are the best and worst stadium or picnic foods.

🔍 REVIEW

- When we <u>evaluate</u>, we determine the worth or value of something.
- We <u>evaluate</u> something when we determine how important it is.
- We study something carefully to <u>evaluate</u> its worth or value.

💬 COLLABORATE

When we look back at what this word means, we see that it means to determine how important or valuable something is.

Use a separate piece of paper to complete these activities:

① Read the prompts below and take notes to record your responses.
- How would you <u>evaluate</u> the importance of stadium food at an event?
- How would you <u>evaluate</u> the pros and cons of offering food for sale at a stadium event?
- <u>Evaluate</u> the problems that arise from limiting outside food at a stadium event.

② Take turns interviewing a partner, asking the questions listed above. Refer to your notes to respond to your partner's questions.

ILLUSTRATE

DEFINE

Question: What does it mean to _illustrate_ something?
Answer: When we _illustrate_ something, we draw pictures for our writing. We use words or pictures as examples to explain something or make it easy to understand.

STUDY

Sample Prompt: What is one way we can _illustrate_ our ideas with words instead of drawings?
Sample Answer: We can use examples to _illustrate_ ideas in writing and to show readers what we mean to say.

Sample Prompt: What example could you give to _illustrate_ how magnetism works?
Sample Answer: I notice that a magnet has a north-pole end and a south-pole end. If I have two magnets and I hold the end of one magnet next to the end of the other magnet, I find that like poles repel and unlike poles attract.

✏ PRACTICE

① **Task:** Research magnets as needed to prepare to write an explanatory paragraph. 🖊

② **Prompt:** Write a paragraph about how magnets work. Use a separate piece of paper.

③ **Prompt:** What examples would _illustrate_ your main points to make them easier for readers to understand?

_____

_____

_____

_____

④ **Task:** _Illustrate_ your writing with a simple sketch or diagram. Include labels as needed to explain your diagram.

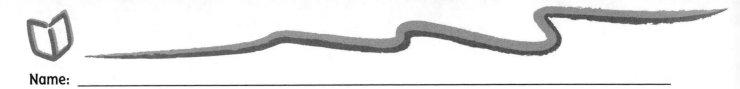

ILLUSTRATE (cont.)

☑ CHECK

Look back at what the word <u>illustrate</u> means.

Use a separate piece of paper to complete these activities:

① Work with a small group to write and <u>illustrate</u> three ways we use principles of magnetism in everyday life.

② <u>Illustrate</u> your writing with specific examples to help readers better understand the topic.

③ How could you add visual elements to <u>illustrate</u> your understanding of how magnetism works?

④ Use technology to prepare your shared writing to present to the rest of the class. Include visual elements. 🖊️

⑤ As a group, present your work to the class.

🔍 REVIEW

· When we <u>illustrate</u> something, we explain it to make it clear.
· We can give an example to <u>illustrate</u> something to make it easy to understand.
· We can <u>illustrate</u> something by adding pictures or drawings to our writing.
· When we <u>illustrate</u> our writing with pictures, it can explain or decorate our writing.

💬 COLLABORATE

When we look back at what this word means, we see that it means to use words or pictures to make something easy to understand.

① Write a paragraph to <u>illustrate</u> an experience you have had with magnetism. Include sensory details to help <u>illustrate</u> your writing. Use a separate piece of paper.

② Trade papers with a partner.

③ Describe how you could use words to <u>illustrate</u> your understanding of your partner's writing. Write your response on your partner's paper.

④ How would you <u>illustrate</u> your partner's writing with a drawing or other visual element?

_____

_____

_____

⑤ <u>Illustrate</u> your partner's paragraph on a separate piece of paper. Give your drawing to your partner and discuss how the visual element adds to the writing.

Name: _____

CONSTRUCT

 DEFINE

Question: What does it mean to <u>construct</u> something?
Answer: When we <u>construct</u> something, we make or create it. We <u>construct</u> a story when we create it by organizing ideas and words.

 STUDY

Sample Prompt: What examples can you find to show you how to <u>construct</u> a fantasy story?
Sample Answer: I can look at fantasy stories other people have written to see how they are <u>constructed</u>. I can study the types of characters, settings, and events in the story to learn how to <u>construct</u> and write a fantasy story.

Sample Prompt: How would you plan to <u>construct</u> a fantasy story?
Sample Answer: I could brainstorm and write notes about certain parts of the story, such as any unusual creatures, magic, or special powers that would be in the story.

✏️ **PRACTICE**

① **Task:** On a separate piece of paper, draw a web to <u>construct</u> a setting for a fantasy story. What words will you use to create a picture in readers' minds of the place where the story happens?

② **Prompt:** What facts or other information will you need to gather to <u>construct</u> your fantasy story?

_____

_____

_____

_____

③ **Task:** What characteristics have you noticed in people you know? Put together characteristics from different people to <u>construct</u> one or more characters for your story. Consider drawing an outline of a person on a separate piece of paper to think about the traits of your main character.

④ **Prompt:** Use your notes from Practice Task #3 to describe your main character.

_____

_____

_____

⑤ **Prompt:** Use your notes from the Practice Tasks and Prompts above to <u>construct</u> a fantasy story. Write your story on a separate piece of paper or use a word-processing program to type your story. ✒️

CONSTRUCT *(cont.)*

☑ CHECK

Look back at what the word <u>construct</u> means.

① Work with a small group to <u>construct</u> a graphic organizer to help classmates <u>construct</u> a fantasy. Use a separate piece of paper.

② What elements need to be included or addressed in the graphic organizer?

③ Discuss the following questions to guide you as you <u>construct</u> the graphic organizer.

- What approach could you use to <u>construct</u> a fantasy story?
- How would you further develop the fantasy story you <u>constructed</u>?
- What is another way you could plan to <u>construct</u> a fantasy story?
- How could you adapt the fantasy story you <u>constructed</u> for a different audience?

🔍 REVIEW

- We create or make something when we <u>construct</u> something.
- When we <u>construct</u> something, we combine or arrange parts to make it.

🗩 COLLABORATE

When we look back at what this word means, we see that it means to arrange words and ideas to create something, such as a story.

① Read the story a classmate wrote for Practice Prompt #5.

② How did your partner portray the main character, setting, and events in the fantasy story he or she <u>constructed</u>?

_____

_____

③ Use your notes from #2 above to provide feedback to your partner about the effectiveness of his or her writing.

④ Ask your partner questions about the story he or she <u>constructed</u>:

- What would happen if…?
- How would you adapt your story to create a different story?
- How could you change the plot to make it more interesting or engaging for readers?

⑤ Predict how the fantasy story your partner <u>constructed</u> might end. Share your ideas with your partner.

Name: _____

CRITICIZE

 DEFINE

Question: What does it mean to <u>criticize</u> something?

Answer: When we <u>criticize</u> something, we point out the good and bad parts in a piece, such as a story, movie, or play. When we <u>criticize</u> writing, we examine and review it.

 STUDY

Sample Prompt: What criteria might you use to <u>criticize</u> a story?

Sample Answer: I could think about the author's purpose and rate the writing based on how well the author met his or her goals in writing the story.

Sample Prompt: How could you <u>criticize</u> writing in a way that helps writers?

Sample Answer: I could give specific examples to show how the author could improve the writing.

 PRACTICE

① **Task:** <u>Criticize</u> a story you have written that you would like to improve. Read the piece to review it.

② **Task:** Use different colors to mark places you could improve your writing. Use the questions below as a guide and mark each aspect of your story with a different color.

- Are there extra words and sentences? Make sure everything is necessary in the story.
- Are the setting, characters, and events in the story believable?
- Does the main character have a clear goal or something he or she wants?
- Does the main character face a conflict or problem that starts him or her on a journey?
- Is there a balance of dialogue and actions to show what happens in the story?

③ **Prompt:** On a separate piece of paper, answer the following questions to further <u>criticize</u> your writing to make your story as effective as possible.

- Which parts work really well and keep your audience reading? Why?
- Which parts might readers have difficulty understanding? Why?
- What is the most important part of the story? Why?
- What is one thing you could do to make your writing stronger?

CRITICIZE (cont.)

☑ CHECK

Look back at what the word <u>criticize</u> means.

① Work with a small group to <u>criticize</u> the story excerpt below.

Tessa tugged on José's jacket sleeve. "Aren't the stunt kites wonderful with their long, swirling tails?" She pointed to a diamond-shaped magenta kite with jewel-toned streamers attached.

"I suppose, but the parafoil kites are pretty awesome, too. I bet they have enough power to lift someone off the sand." He stuck his hands in his pockets and sauntered down the beach, looking carefully at all the kites on display. The weather was perfect for the kite festival, with plenty of wind and a few scattered clouds.

A sudden gust of wind whipped the nearby banners into a frenzy and snatched the tails of anything flying in the air. Threatening gray clouds moved quickly toward shore and spit a few drops onto José and Tessa.

"We'd better run for cover!" Tessa grabbed José's hand and pulled him behind her as she scrambled up the sand bank. They headed for nearby vendors' tents, reaching one just as a cloudburst drenched anyone standing in the open.

José glanced with interest around the booth that sheltered them. Displays of every imaginable kind of head covering swayed in the wind. While they waited for the squall to pass, he encouraged Tessa to try on one silly hat after another.

Use a separate piece of paper to complete these activities:

② What details can you use to support the comments you made when you <u>criticized</u> the writing?

③ What do you think the author should have done differently? Why?

④ <u>Criticize</u> the value or importance of this piece of writing.

🔍 REVIEW

· When we <u>criticize</u> something, we evaluate its good and bad points.

· When we <u>criticize</u> a written piece, we examine and review it.

💬 COLLABORATE

When we look back at what this word means, we see that it means to examine and review the good and bad points in a written work.

Use a separate piece of paper to complete these activities:

① Work with a partner to create a list of questions you could use to <u>criticize</u> a written work.

② Your teacher will provide each pair of students with an anonymous sample of student writing. Ask the questions you wrote in #1 to <u>criticize</u> the writing. ✒️

③ Discuss how you answered your questions to <u>criticize</u> a written work.

Name: _____

INCORPORATE

 DEFINE

Question: What does it mean to <u>incorporate</u> something?

Answer: When we <u>incorporate</u> something, we make it part of something else. We unite or combine things to form a single whole when we <u>incorporate</u> something.

 STUDY

Sample Prompt: What features do planners often <u>incorporate</u> into tourist attractions?

Sample Answer: Planners <u>incorporate</u> features that make the site accessible for visitors, services that allow people to participate in activities, and advertising to let people know the attraction exists.

Sample Prompt: How might tourism professionals use a model to consider which features to <u>incorporate</u> into tourist attractions?

Sample Answer: Professionals might study existing tourist attractions to evaluate the effectiveness of specific features.

 PRACTICE

① **Prompt:** What type of tourist attraction do you most like to visit? What features does it <u>incorporate</u> that make the site interesting to you?

_____

_____

② **Prompt:** Which characteristics do you believe are most important to <u>incorporate</u> into tourist attractions? Include your reasons for each characteristic or feature.

_____

_____

③ **Prompt:** What would you <u>incorporate</u> into a tourist attraction to address environmental concerns and maintain natural resources?

_____

_____

④ **Prompt:** How would you <u>incorporate</u> the features you described in Practice Prompts #2 and #3 into a tourist attraction?

_____

_____

INCORPORATE (cont.)

☑ CHECK

Look back at what the word <u>incorporate</u> means.

① Your teacher will assign a particular type of tourist attraction to your small group. [/]

② Use a dictionary and other resources to define your assigned tourist attraction.

Use a separate piece of paper to complete these activities:

③ Work together to brainstorm a list of factors to consider when determining what to <u>incorporate</u> into your assigned tourist attraction.

④ What features would you <u>incorporate</u> into this tourist attraction?

⑤ Share your work with the rest of the class.

⑥ Work together as a whole class to complete a chart similar to the sample on the right to show features we <u>incorporate</u> into different types of tourist attractions.

Geophysical/ Landscape Attractions	Ecological/Biological Attractions
Cultural/Historical Attractions	Recreational Attractions

🔍 REVIEW

· When we <u>incorporate</u> something, we put it with something that already exists to make a unified whole.

· We include something as part of something else when we <u>incorporate</u> it.

· We include something or work it into the whole when we <u>incorporate</u> it.

💬 COLLABORATE

When we look back at what this word means, we see that it means to include something as part of a unified whole.

① Read the paragraph below with a classmate. Use a separate piece of paper to answer the questions.

Walt Disney World is truly a world of tourist attractions. This area includes the Magic Kingdom and Epcot, as well as other theme parks and water parks. The Magic Kingdom includes classic Disney attractions, similar to the original Disneyland. Epcot allows visitors to experience showcase activities from countries around the world. Theme parks include Hollywood- and animal-themed activities. The resort offers shuttles between parks and packages for visitors who want to experience multiple attractions.

② Research and discuss with your partner to gather additional information about this tourist attraction. [/]

③ Which features did planners <u>incorporate</u> into this tourist attraction?

④ What other features do you think should be <u>incorporated</u> into this attraction?

Name: _____

INTERPRET

 DEFINE

Question: What does it mean to interpret something?
Answer: When we interpret something, we decide what it means. We can use facts, details, or events to interpret the meaning of something and explain or tell what it means. Sometimes we tell what we believe about something.

 STUDY

Sample Prompt: How would you interpret the importance of following the rules to play outdoor games?
Sample Answer: Outdoor games have rules to keep the playing experience safe and fair for everyone.

Sample Prompt: How would you interpret this quotation?

"Don't change the rules in the middle of the game." ~ English proverb

Sample Answer: One way to interpret this quotation is to take it at face value. A game is more fair and easier for everyone to play if the rules established at the beginning are followed throughout the game.

PRACTICE

① **Prompt:** How do people use facts and details to interpret rules when they are learning to play a new game?

_____

_____

_____

② **Prompt:** Give examples to interpret how knowing the rules to one outdoor game might help you learn to play a different game.

_____

_____

_____

③ **Prompt:** How would you interpret the rules for keeping score in an outdoor game you like to play? Why is keeping score important in this game?

_____

_____

_____

_____

INTERPRET *(cont.)*

☑ CHECK

Look back at what the word <u>interpret</u> means.

① Work with a small group to define and understand how figurative language works. Consider these questions:

- What are some examples of figurative language?
- How do people <u>interpret</u> the meaning of figurative language?

② Write samples of figurative language together with your group. Use a separate piece of paper.

③ Work together to create a game with your figurative language samples. Write rules for how to play your game. Make sure your game rules would be easy for others to <u>interpret</u> so they will be able to play your game. Use a separate piece of paper.

④ Trade games with another group in the class.

⑤ <u>Interpret</u> the rules the other group wrote to play their game.

🔍 REVIEW

- When we <u>interpret</u> something, we explain or tell what it means.
- We can use facts and details to <u>interpret</u> something.
- When we <u>interpret</u> something, we tell our understanding of it based on our beliefs and judgments about it.
- We might use what happened to <u>interpret</u> what something means.

🗩 COLLABORATE

When we look back at what this word means, we see that it means to decide and tell what something means.

Use a separate piece of paper to complete these activities:

① Take turns with a classmate <u>interpreting</u> how to play your favorite video game. Refer to the questions below to guide you.

- What is the main idea of the game?
- How would you describe players' actions during the game?
- What happens if _____?
- How would you compare or contrast this game with other games to help someone <u>interpret</u> how to play it?

② Give examples to <u>interpret</u> the rules for your partner.

③ Ask questions and give feedback to your partner to show you <u>interpreted</u> his or her explanation of the game rules correctly.

Name: _____

JUSTIFY

 DEFINE

Question: What does it mean to <u>justify</u>?

Answer: When we <u>justify</u>, we give a reason or explanation that makes sense to show that something is reasonable. We might <u>justify</u> an action by giving reasons or explaining why it makes sense.

 STUDY

Sample Prompt: <u>Justify</u> the value and importance of using online materials to research a topic of interest.

Sample Answer: Online materials offer a wider variety than print materials, since the Internet covers a much broader geographic area than a physical library. When we research online, we can read a wide variety of sources about a topic.

Sample Prompt: <u>Justify</u> why people might choose to read ebooks.

Sample Answer: People read ebooks because often the price is less expensive. It is easy to take an ebook with you on an electronic device.

✎ **PRACTICE**

① **Prompt:** How would you choose to research a topic of interest? Would you visit a public library? Would you look at a digital library website online? Would you read paper books and articles? Would you research articles and other websites online? How would you <u>justify</u> your choice? Write your responses on a separate piece of paper.

② **Prompt:** Which facts would help you <u>justify</u> a decision to visit a public library?

_____

_____

_____

③ **Prompt:** How would you explain and <u>justify</u> the changing roles of the public library in your community?

_____

_____

_____

④ **Prompt:** Refer to your responses to Practice Prompts #1–3 to write a letter to your city council to <u>justify</u> maintaining and improving the public library in your community. If your community does not have a public library, write to someone in the school district to <u>justify</u> maintaining and improving your school library. Use a separate piece of paper.

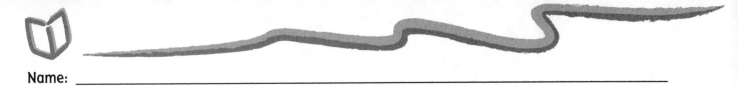

Name: _____

JUSTIFY *(cont.)*

☑ CHECK

Look back at what the word <u>justify</u> means.

For purposes of this lesson, "public library" refers to a library housed in a physical building and "digital library" refers to a library website.

① Work together as a class to explore and <u>justify</u> the role of digital libraries in student learning. Answer these questions on a separate piece of paper:

- How would you define and explain a digital library?
- What services might such a library offer?

② What reasons might a student have for using a digital library instead of a public library?

_____

_____

③ How and why would you <u>justify</u> using a digital library to someone else?

_____

_____

④ As a class, use technology to create a brochure to <u>justify</u> and explain features of a local library's website.

○ REVIEW

- When we <u>justify</u> something, we show that it is right or reasonable.
- When we <u>justify</u> an answer, we provide a good reason for it.
- We can <u>justify</u> a response by giving reasons to prove that it makes sense.
- We can <u>justify</u> an action by giving a reason or explanation to show that it makes sense.

💬 COLLABORATE

When we look back at what this word means, we see that it means to give reasons to show that something is right or reasonable.

Use a separate piece of paper to complete these activities:

① Work with a classmate to create a list of criteria to <u>justify</u> why students should read paper books.

② What factors will you consider in <u>justifying</u> reasons why students should read paper books?

③ How would you <u>justify</u> the role and importance of paper books in today's society?

④ Present your criteria and reasons to another pair of students.

Name: _____

DISTINGUISH

 ## DEFINE

Question: What does it mean to <u>distinguish</u> between two or more things or ideas?

Answer: When we <u>distinguish</u> between two or more things or ideas, we tell the difference between them. We can separate things or ideas into groups to think about how they are different.

 ## STUDY

Sample Prompt: How would you <u>distinguish</u> between a hen and a rooster?

Sample Answer: Hens lay eggs, and roosters crow. In general, roosters have larger combs and waddles, and their tail feathers are fuller and pointed.

Sample Prompt: Why is it important to <u>distinguish</u> between dairy farming and cattle ranching?

Sample Answer: We <u>distinguish</u> between these two types of businesses to better understand where our food comes from. Dairy farmers harvest milk from their cattle, and ranchers raise cattle for beef. Each type of business follows its own schedule and has its own duties.

PRACTICE

① **Prompt:** How can you <u>distinguish</u> between different types of horses?

_____

_____

_____

② **Prompt:** Why might you want or need to <u>distinguish</u> between different types of horses?

_____

_____

_____

③ **Prompt:** How might you <u>distinguish</u> fact from fiction in a story about horses?

_____

_____

_____

④ **Prompt:** On a separate piece of paper, write a story about horses. Include facts and details to <u>distinguish</u> the specific type of horse in your story and use that information to support what happens in your story.

Name: _____

DISTINGUISH (cont.)

☑ CHECK

Look back at what the word <u>distinguish</u> means.

① Work with a small group to create categories to <u>distinguish</u> between different farm animals.

② Create a chart to identify your categories and which animals belong to each category, including reasons to explain how you <u>distinguished</u> between animals. Use a separate piece of paper.

③ Share your chart with another group of classmates. Then discuss these questions with your group:

- How did your classmates choose to <u>distinguish</u> animals? What are the similarities and differences between the ways you categorized groups of animals?

- How might someone working with farm animals use this information?

⚲ REVIEW

- We can <u>distinguish</u> between two or more things or people by thinking about how they are different.

- We might separate things into groups by their differences to <u>distinguish</u> between them.

- We <u>distinguish</u> when we recognize how one thing or person is different from other things and people.

💬 COLLABORATE

When we look back at what this word means, we see that it means to notice the differences between two or more things or ideas.

① With a classmate, read the paragraph below.

When people visualize animals on a farm, they often include a dog in their mental pictures. Those who work on a farm select a dog based on the function they want the dog to perform. Working dogs guard and protect livestock. Within this group, some breeds have thick coats that enable them to withstand the cold while out in the fields. Another group of dogs has natural herding instincts. They often serve important roles on a working farm with livestock. Hunting dogs often also make good companion dogs. These dogs may be trained to be loyal members of the family.

② Discuss with your partner how you could <u>distinguish</u> between the types of dogs that live and work on farms.

③ How would you <u>distinguish</u> between the different purposes farm dogs might fulfill as described in the paragraph? Use a separate piece of paper.

④ What specific characteristics would you expect each type of farm dog to have? Use the same separate piece of paper.

Name: _____

DIFFERENTIATE

 DEFINE

Question: What does it mean to <u>differentiate</u>?

Answer: When we <u>differentiate</u>, we understand the differences between things. We see or state the differences between two or more things.

 STUDY

Sample Prompt: How would you <u>differentiate</u> between singing and speaking?

Sample Answer: When someone is speaking, he or she makes sure a listener can understand the words. The speaker varies the pitch, tone, and speed to convey his or her message. A singer follows a composer's written directions for pitch, tone, and speed.

Sample Prompt: How might a group of musicians <u>differentiate</u> their instruments in an orchestra in which more than one person plays the same instrument?

Sample Answer: A musician can <u>differentiate</u> his or her instrument by labeling it or putting a sticker on the instrument case.

✏️ **PRACTICE**

① **Prompt:** Think about a concert you have attended or another event where you listened to music. How would you <u>differentiate</u> the type of music you heard from other types of music?

_____

_____

② **Prompt:** Write a narrative about the concert or musical event you described in Practice Prompt #1.

_____

_____

_____

_____

_____

③ **Task:** Share your story with a classmate. How would you <u>differentiate</u> between the types of music you each described?

_____

_____

Name: _____

DIFFERENTIATE (cont.)

☑ CHECK

Look back at what the word <u>differentiate</u> means.

① Work together as a class to <u>differentiate</u> between types of musical instruments.

② How is one group of musical instruments different from another? Use print or online images and definitions to <u>differentiate</u> between groups of musical instruments. 📝

③ What characteristics and qualities <u>differentiate</u> one group of musical instruments from another group?

_____

_____

④ Use your background knowledge as well as what you heard in the class discussion to write a clue about a musical instrument. Use a separate piece of paper.

⑤ Share your clue with classmates and invite them to <u>differentiate</u> between musical instruments to guess the musical instrument you described in your clue.

🔍 REVIEW

- We understand how things are different when we <u>differentiate</u> between them.
- We <u>differentiate</u> between things by marking or showing how they are different.
- We can <u>differentiate</u> by stating the differences between things.

💬 COLLABORATE

When we look back at what this word means, we see that it means to identify and understand the differences between things.

Use a separate piece of paper to complete these activities:

① Discuss with a partner other action words you have studied and practiced that have meanings similar to <u>differentiate</u>. Use a print or online thesaurus as needed. 📝

② Review the meanings of the words you mentioned.

③ How does reviewing nuances in word meanings help you <u>differentiate</u> between these words?

④ How can understanding what specific words mean help you better complete classroom activities that include these action words?

⑤ Work together to write a sample sentence for each word. Each sentence will direct readers to do a task or activity based on the meaning of each word.

Name: _____

PERSUADE

 DEFINE

Question: What does it mean to <u>persuade</u> someone?

Answer: When we <u>persuade</u> someone, we make someone do or believe something. We do this by giving that person good reasons to do or believe what we say.

 STUDY

Sample Prompt: What are things we can do to <u>persuade</u> someone to agree with our opinion about social media?

Sample Answer: We can consider the opinion from the audience's perspective and write to overcome any objections that might be expressed.

Sample Prompt: What reasons would you give to <u>persuade</u> a teacher to allow students to use social media, such as Pinterest, in the classroom?

Sample Answer: Students could use the site to post their projects for peer review, make comments, and participate in class discussions. Teachers could gather and post images related to a particular topic of study.

✎ **PRACTICE**

① **Prompt:** What is your opinion about students owning cell phones? How would you <u>persuade</u> someone to agree with your opinion?

_____

_____

_____

② **Prompt:** What is the most important factor to consider in an argument to <u>persuade</u> an adult to allow a student to own a cell phone? Why is this factor important?

_____

_____

_____

③ **Prompt:** What facts and details would you use to <u>persuade</u> someone to use social media?

_____

_____

_____

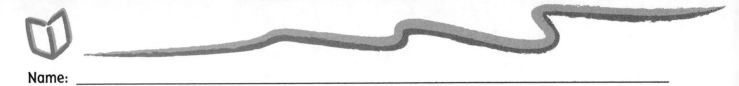

PERSUADE (cont.)

☑ CHECK

Look back at what the word <u>persuade</u> means.

① Discuss with classmates ways in which social media <u>persuades</u> people. Consider these questions:
- How does social media <u>persuade</u> people to do or think something in particular?
- Why does social media try to <u>persuade</u> people?

② Work with classmates to identify a specific example of how social media <u>persuades</u> people to believe or do something in particular.

Use a separate piece of paper to complete these activities:

③ List the reasons given for the opinion expressed about social media in your example.

④ Create a general list of tips or suggestions to help peers when they feel pressured or <u>persuaded</u> by social media.

⑤ Share your suggestions with another class and/or create a poster to display in your school.

🔍 REVIEW

- We <u>persuade</u> someone by giving good reasons to do or believe something.
- We <u>persuade</u> someone when we convince them to do or believe something.
- We can <u>persuade</u> someone to do something by asking them sincerely.

💬 COLLABORATE

When we look back at what this word means, we see that it means to give reasons for someone to believe or do something.

① What role should social media play in the daily lives of you and your classmates? How would you <u>persuade</u> a teacher, parent, or other family member to agree with your opinion?

_____

_____

_____

② Share your thoughts with a partner. Discuss the problem(s) you might face in <u>persuading</u> someone to agree with your opinion. How might you overcome any objections?

③ Share your insights on how you and your partner would <u>persuade</u> an adult to agree with your opinion about the role of social media in your daily life.

Name: _____

COMPOSE

DEFINE

Question: What does it mean to <u>compose</u>?
Answer: When we <u>compose</u>, we form something by putting it together. We can <u>compose</u> our thoughts to write something, such as a poem. We <u>compose</u> when we produce pages of type.

STUDY

Sample Prompt: What are different ways you could <u>compose</u> a message to send to a pen pal?
Sample Answer: I could write or type a letter to mail, or I could send an email.

Sample Prompt: Why do we <u>compose</u> something in writing to share with a pen pal?
Sample Answer: A pen pal might be someone we do not know, so we would not text or call that person.

✏️ PRACTICE

① **Prompt:** What are some benefits to corresponding with a pen pal?

_____

_____

_____

② **Prompt:** What is one topic you would suggest for a peer <u>composing</u> a letter to a pen pal?

_____

_____

_____

③ **Prompt:** What details would you include if you were <u>composing</u> a letter to introduce yourself to a pen pal?

_____

_____

_____

④ **Prompt:** If you were <u>composing</u> a letter to a pen pal, what questions could you ask to show interest in your pen pal and get to know him or her better?

_____

_____

_____

COMPOSE (cont.)

☑ CHECK

Look back at what the word <u>compose</u> means.

① As a class, discuss what it means to be a pen pal.

② How would you set up a pen-pal program to give students the opportunity to <u>compose</u> letters and receive responses to their letters?

_____

_____

③ What details would need to be in place for the pen-pal program to be effective?

_____

_____

🔍 REVIEW

- We <u>compose</u> something when we write a poem or another piece of writing.
- We <u>compose</u> when we produce pages of type.
- When we form something by putting it together, we <u>compose</u> something.

💬 COLLABORATE

When we look back at what this word means, we see that it means to put thoughts together to write something.

① Your teacher will suggest recipients for the letters you <u>compose</u>, such as senior citizens, a children's hospital ward, or community-service workers. [✐]

② With a classmate, discuss possible topics you could write about when you <u>compose</u> your letters.

③ <u>Compose</u> a letter to a recipient from the audience your teacher suggested. Use a separate piece of paper.

④ Work with your partner to edit the letter you <u>composed</u> to send to a pen pal. How could you improve your letter to make it more interesting or easier to understand?

_____

_____

⑤ Give and receive feedback about drawings or other illustrations you could include with your letter.

⑥ Send the letter you <u>composed</u> to the intended audience.

79

Name: _____

OUTLINE

 DEFINE

Question: What does it mean to <u>outline</u>?
Answer: When we <u>outline</u>, we write the main points about something. We <u>outline</u> to show only the most important parts. We can also draw a line to <u>outline</u> or show the edge of something.

 STUDY

Sample Prompt: What can I do before I <u>outline</u> to help me get started?
Sample Answer: I can brainstorm and group ideas into categories before I <u>outline</u> a topic.

Sample Prompt: What should I include when I <u>outline</u> a topic?
Sample Answer: When I <u>outline</u> a topic, I should include a word or phrase for each idea that supports a main point.

✏️ **PRACTICE**

① **Task:** What is a country you would like to learn more about? Research this country and take notes on a separate piece of paper. <u>Outline</u> important information and facts you might include in a report. 🖊️

② **Prompt:** <u>Outline</u> the main points for your report about the country you researched.

_____

_____

_____

③ **Prompt:** <u>Outline</u> the points you want to include about the way people live in this country.

_____

_____

_____

④ **Prompt:** How would you <u>outline</u> information about the climate in your chosen country?

_____

_____

_____

⑤ **Prompt:** Use the main points and details you <u>outlined</u> to write a complete report about this country. Use a separate piece of paper.

Name: _____

OUTLINE (cont.)

☑ CHECK

Look back at what the word <u>outline</u> means.

① Discuss with classmates what you know about forms of government in different countries.

② Research as needed to understand how government works in different places. 📝

③ Work together as a class to create a graphic organizer to <u>outline</u> different forms of government. Use a separate piece of paper. Display your completed graphic organizer on a bulletin board.

🔍 REVIEW

· We <u>outline</u> our ideas for a topic when we list the main points we will write about.

· We can <u>outline</u> to list or show only the most important parts of something.

· We <u>outline</u> when we draw a line that shows the edge of something.

💬 COLLABORATE

When we look back at what this word means, we see that it means to write the main points about something.

① Share with a classmate the information you <u>outlined</u> about a country in Practice Prompts #2, #3, and #4.

② Give and receive feedback about additional points you could <u>outline</u> to make your finished piece more interesting for readers. Consider these questions:

· How did your partner organize information when he or she <u>outlined</u> the topic?

· How well did your partner incorporate background knowledge and research when he or she <u>outlined</u> the topic?

· What is another way you or your partner could <u>outline</u> the information about your country?

DRAFT

 DEFINE

Question: What does it mean to <u>draft</u> something?

Answer: When we <u>draft</u> something, we make a first, rough copy of it. We <u>draft</u> when we draw a preliminary sketch or plan of something.

 STUDY

Sample Prompt: Why do we first <u>draft</u> something we want to write?

Sample Answer: This step helps us get thoughts onto paper. When we don't stop to make sure everything is perfect, our ideas flow more smoothly.

Sample Prompt: When someone <u>drafts</u> a tall tale, what might he or she include?

Sample Answer: When drafting a tall tale, a person might include events that seem unlikely or impossible. The story would be exaggerated.

✎ **PRACTICE**

① **Prompt:** What is one thing to consider when <u>drafting</u> a tall tale?

_____

_____

② **Prompt:** What have you already learned about outlining that might help you <u>draft</u> a tall tale?

_____

_____

_____

③ **Task:** On a separate piece of paper, brainstorm concrete words and sensory details to include when you <u>draft</u> your tall tale.

④ **Prompt:** <u>Draft</u> a list of possible events for your tall tale.

_____

_____

_____

_____

⑤ **Prompt:** Refer to your responses in Practice Prompts #1 and #4 and Practice Task #3 to <u>draft</u> a tall tale. Use a separate piece of paper.

DRAFT (cont.)

☑ CHECK

Look back at what the word <u>draft</u> means.

① What do you know about tall tales? <u>Draft</u> a response on a separate piece of paper.

② Share your ideas with classmates.

③ As a class, research tall tales to learn more about this genre. 🖊

④ Work together in a small group to <u>draft</u> an informative essay about tall tales. Use a separate piece of paper.

🔍 REVIEW

- When we <u>draft</u>, we create the first version of something.
- We might <u>draft</u> a drawing or plan of something to show what the final version will be like.

💬 COLLABORATE

When we look back at what this word means, we see that it means to write the first, rough copy of something.

① With a classmate, read the version of a tall tale <u>drafted</u> below.

Paul Bunyan, a legendary logging hero, had little in the way of earthly possessions. But he did own Babe, a big blue ox. They say Babe was seven axe handles wide between the eyes. Others say he was forty-two axe handles wide. Either measurement would be correct, since seven of Paul's axe handles equaled forty-two of anyone else's. Paul used Babe to haul logs off 640 acres at a time and to pull the kinks out of the crooked logging roads. The downside is no one could keep Babe for more than one night at camp. The amount of food the ox would eat in a day would feed the camp men for a year. He snacked on fifty bales of hay at a time, wire and all. When he wasn't eating or working, Babe did cause mischief on occasion, but Paul still considered him a great pet.

② Discuss the tall tale with your partner. What do you notice? Consider these questions:
- Which parts could be reworded to make the meaning clearer for readers?
- Which ideas could be further developed?
- How could the author use figurative language or idioms to convey the sense of a tall tale?

③ Work together to <u>draft</u> your own version of this tall tale. Use a separate piece of paper.

④ As time allows, share with the class the version you <u>drafted</u>.

Name: _____

EDIT

DEFINE

Question: What does it mean to edit?

Answer: When we edit, we check a piece of writing to make sure the spelling, grammar, and facts are correct. We also edit when we take out extra words. When we edit a piece of writing, we prepare it for publication.

STUDY

Sample Prompt: What is one strategy we can use to start editing our writing?

Sample Answer: Reading our writing aloud can help us catch mistakes or other things that may need to be changed.

Sample Prompt: How can a checklist help us edit our writing?

Sample Answer: A checklist reminds us of things to look for that may need to be corrected or changed in our writing.

PRACTICE

① **Prompt:** Why is it important to edit our writing?

_____

_____

_____

② **Task:** Edit the paragraph below.

People have observed the weather for hundreds of years. They notice weather pattern, which help them make predictions about future weather. People use instruments to observe and forecast weather. these instruments include thermometers, rain gauges, and barometers. Some wether instruments, such as radar, are more sophisticated. However, Human observation still plays an important role in weather forecasting. Anyone can observe sky conditions types of clouds, and type of precipitation.

③ **Prompt:** What are specific ways editing would strengthen the writing above and make it easier for the audience to read and understand?

_____

_____

_____

Name: _____

EDIT *(cont.)*

☑ CHECK

Look back at what the word <u>edit</u> means.

① Discuss with a small group why it is often difficult to <u>edit</u> your writing.

② Identify specific things to look for when you <u>edit</u> your own or someone else's writing.

③ Work together to create a checklist for <u>editing</u> an informative paragraph. Use a separate piece of paper and consider these questions:

- What specific things would you check?
- What might need to be changed when you <u>edit</u> this type of writing?

🔍 REVIEW

- When we <u>edit</u> our writing, we make changes and correct mistakes.
- We <u>edit</u> writing to prepare it to be published.

💬 COLLABORATE

When we look back at what this word means, we see that it means to revise and correct writing to get it ready for publication.

① Write a paragraph about weather forecasting or tools you have used to observe the weather.

_____

_____

_____

_____

_____

_____

② How could you help a partner <u>edit</u> his or her writing?

_____

_____

_____

③ Work with your partner to help each other <u>edit</u> your writing. Remember to say something positive about your partner's writing as well as suggesting changes.

Name: _____

MODEL

DEFINE

Question: What does it mean to <u>model</u> something?
Answer: When we <u>model</u> something, we set an example for others to follow. We can also <u>model</u> by following a pattern to plan or make something.

STUDY

Sample Prompt: How can we <u>model</u> something for someone else?
Sample Answer: We <u>model</u> by showing someone how to do something and telling them what to notice about the procedure.

Sample Prompt: What are important factors to consider when you <u>model</u> how to do something?
Sample Answer: <u>Model</u> details that show how to do the procedure and explain reasons for the actions.

✎ PRACTICE

① **Prompt:** What science experiment using force and motion could you <u>model</u> for classmates?

_____

_____

_____

_____

② **Prompt:** What have you observed someone else <u>model</u> that will help you design and plan your science experiment?

_____

_____

_____

_____

③ **Prompt:** How would you organize the parts of your experiment to <u>model</u> it for classmates?

_____

_____

_____

_____

④ **Prompt:** List the actions you would take to <u>model</u> the experiment. Use a separate piece of paper.

Name: _____

MODEL *(cont.)*

☑ CHECK

Look back at what the word <u>model</u> means.

① Observe as your teacher <u>models</u> constructing a design for a go-cart. As a class, answer the questions below. 📝

- What do you notice about the procedure your teacher <u>modeled</u>?

- What will you be expected to do when you <u>model</u> the activity?

② Work with a small group to <u>model</u> the same procedure to construct a design for a go-cart.

③ What problems might you face as you design a go-cart, and how will you solve those problems? Write your answers on a separate piece of paper.

④ How might you <u>model</u> your solutions for other groups who face the same problems? Use the same separate piece of paper.

⑤ Listen and apply feedback from your teacher as you <u>model</u> constructing a design for a go-cart.

⑥ Discuss with your small group how you could use what you have learned about force and motion to <u>model</u> an experiment with a completed go-cart.

🔍 REVIEW

- When we <u>model</u> something, we follow a pattern to plan or make something.
- When we <u>model</u> something, we design something that is similar to something else.
- We can imitate the form of something when we <u>model</u>.

💬 COLLABORATE

When we look back at what this word means, we see that it means to set an example or follow a pattern to create something.

Use a separate piece of paper to complete these activities:

① Discuss with a classmate an approach you could use to <u>model</u> constructing and flying a paper airplane.

② How would you <u>model</u> the effects of force and gravity?

③ What facts, details, and other information would you incorporate to <u>model</u> a science experiment with a paper airplane?

④ Work together to write a plan to describe how you would <u>model</u> your experiment for classmates.

Name: _____

CLASSIFY

 DEFINE

Question: What does it mean to <u>classify</u> things?
Answer: When we <u>classify</u> things, we put them into groups according to their characteristics.

 STUDY

Sample Prompt: Why is it important to <u>classify</u> items for recycling?
Sample Answer: When items are <u>classified</u> before they reach a recycling center, it saves time, energy, and resources in the recycling process.

Sample Prompt: What characteristics or criteria do people use to <u>classify</u> metal items for recycling?
Sample Answer: People <u>classify</u> metal items based on the type of metal to recycle them into similar products made from each type of metal.

✎ **PRACTICE**

① **Prompt:** How would you <u>classify</u> items to recycle?

_____

_____

_____

_____

② **Prompt:** How would you demonstrate to someone else how to <u>classify</u> items for recycling?

_____

_____

_____

_____

③ **Task:** On a separate piece of paper, draw a diagram to illustrate your explanation in Practice Prompt #2 of how to <u>classify</u> items for recycling.

④ **Prompt:** What might be the result if an item was <u>classified</u> into the wrong group?

_____

_____

_____

_____

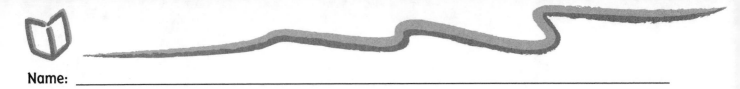

Name: _____

CLASSIFY *(cont.)*

☑ CHECK

Look back at what the word <u>classify</u> means.

① Discuss with a small group your personal experiences in <u>classifying</u> plastic items for recycling. Consider these questions:

- Why do we <u>classify</u> plastic items for recycling?
- What obstacles did you face when you <u>classified</u> plastic items for recycling?

Use a separate piece of paper to complete these activities:

② How would you design a procedure to help others <u>classify</u> plastic items for recycling?

③ What problems might someone face when they <u>classify</u> plastic items for recycling? What would you suggest to solve those problems?

④ Work together to create a graphic organizer, poster, or other visual display to help others <u>classify</u> plastic items for recycling.

⑤ Present your visual display to classmates.

⑥ Share one thing you learned about <u>classifying</u> plastic items for recycling with a friend or family member to help him or her <u>classify</u> such items at home.

🔍 REVIEW

- When we <u>classify</u> things, we arrange them into groups based on ways they are alike.
- We <u>classify</u> something when we consider that it belongs to a certain group.
- We can use what we know about the characteristics of things to <u>classify</u> them into groups.

💬 COLLABORATE

When we look back at what this word means, we see that it means to group things by their characteristics.

① Work with a classmate to research ways different communities <u>classify</u> items for recycling.

② What specific examples can you find of ways different communities <u>classify</u> items for recycling?

_____

_____

_____

③ Discuss with your partner how you might apply what you learned to <u>classify</u> items for recycling at home or at school.

SUMMARIZE

DEFINE

Question: What does it mean to <u>summarize</u>?

Answer: When we <u>summarize</u>, we give a short statement that tells the main ideas of something. We can <u>summarize</u> something that has been said or written. When we <u>summarize</u>, we decide what is most important.

STUDY

Sample Prompt: What is one reason we might <u>summarize</u> a text?

Sample Answer: When we <u>summarize</u>, it helps us reflect on the meaning of what we read.

Sample Prompt: How would you <u>summarize</u> the sky phenomenon called a "shooting star"?

Sample Answer: A "shooting star" is really a meteoroid falling into Earth's atmosphere and burning up. When it falls, it produces a trail of light we call a *meteor*.

✎ PRACTICE

① **Task:** Use available print and online resources to research polar lights (*aurora polaris*). On a separate piece of paper, take notes to gather information and provide a list of sources. 🖊

② **Prompt:** <u>Summarize</u> what you read in the box below.

[ ]

③ **Prompt:** What conclusions do you draw from <u>summarizing</u> your research?

_____

_____

_____

_____

④ **Prompt:** On a separate piece of paper, write a story based on the information you <u>summarized</u> in Practice Prompt #2.

SUMMARIZE (cont.)

☑ CHECK

Look back at what the word <u>summarize</u> means.

① Follow along as your teacher reads the paragraph below. 📝

Sometimes people see flashes of light before or during an earthquake. When an earthquake happens, the geologic stress releases electric charges from certain types of rocks. Earthquake lightning can be different colors. Sometimes the light appears as bluish flames a few inches above the ground. Another form, ball lightning, appears to float in the air for several seconds. Quick flashes of bright light that look like lightning may come out of the ground and stretch toward the sky. Scientists will continue to study these lights to understand if they might play a role in the future to help us predict earthquakes.

② Discuss the questions below with classmates.

- <u>Summarize</u> the main idea of the paragraph.
- Which facts or details did you refer to when you <u>summarized</u> the main idea?
- How did you decide which facts or details were most important to <u>summarize</u> the information in the paragraph?

③ Work with a small group to <u>summarize</u> the connections you can make after reading the paragraph. What connections can you make between the text and your life? between this text and other texts? between the text and local or global communities? Write your group's answers on a separate piece of paper.

🔍 REVIEW

- We <u>summarize</u> when we give a short statement that tells the main ideas of something.
- We can <u>summarize</u> something that has been said or written.
- Sometimes people <u>summarize</u> ideas that have been said in a group.

🗩 COLLABORATE

When we look back at what this word means, we see that it means to say or write the main idea of something briefly.

① Read a classmate's response for Practice Prompt #4. <u>Summarize</u> what you read and communicate it to your partner.

② How would you <u>summarize</u> the meaning of the story? <u>Summarize</u> the theme and restate it in your own words to your partner.

RECITE

 ## DEFINE

Question: What does it mean to <u>recite</u>?
Answer: When we <u>recite</u>, we say aloud something we have memorized. When we read something aloud, we <u>recite</u>. We <u>recite</u> when we tell about something in detail. We <u>recite</u> when we answer questions about a lesson.

 ## STUDY

Sample Prompt: Why do people learn poems to <u>recite</u>?
Sample Answer: Reading and <u>reciting</u> poetry helps us understand emotion, description, and effective word choice, which we can apply to our writing.

Sample Prompt: What do we practice when we <u>recite</u> poetry or other written pieces?
Sample Answer: We practice speaking skills such as diction, expression, and fluency.

PRACTICE

① **Prompt:** Which poems, songs, or other verses have you heard someone <u>recite</u>?

_____

_____

② **Prompt:** How could you learn a poem to <u>recite</u> for others? What steps would you take to learn the poem?

_____

_____

_____

_____

③ **Prompt:** How would you choose which poem to learn and <u>recite</u>?

_____

_____

④ **Prompt:** Who would you like to <u>recite</u> a poem for and why?

_____

_____

⑤ **Task:** Choose a poem you would like to <u>recite</u>. Become familiar with the poem and memorize it, if possible.

RECITE *(cont.)*

☑ CHECK

Look back at what the word recite means.

① Listen as your teacher reads or recites a piece aloud to the class. 📝

② In a small group, take turns reciting a phrase that stood out to you when you heard the piece recited.

③ Take turns reciting details about the piece to better understand its meaning.

④ Recite reasons why the narrator might have chosen specific words to convey details in the piece.

⑤ Write questions about those details and about the meaning of the piece. Use a separate piece of paper.

⑥ Trade questions with another small group.

⑦ Take turns reciting the answers to your classmates' questions.

🔍 REVIEW

- We recite when we repeat something from memory.
- When we recite, we read something aloud in public.
- We recite when we tell about something in detail.
- We might recite facts about something in particular.

💬 COLLABORATE

When we look back at what this word means, we see that it means to say something from memory or read aloud something in public.

① Practice reciting to a classmate the poem you studied in Practice Task #5.

② Compare the pieces you and your partner recited. What did you like about the piece your partner recited?

_____

_____

③ How did hearing the piece your partner recited aloud affect you? How do you think its effect would change if you read the piece silently?

_____

_____

④ As time allows, discuss with your partner your responses to Practice Prompts #2 and #3.

Name: _____

PARAPHRASE

 ## DEFINE

Question: What does it mean to <u>paraphrase</u>?
Answer: When we <u>paraphrase</u>, we restate in different words what someone said or wrote. We convey the same meaning using different words when we <u>paraphrase</u>.

 ## STUDY

Sample Prompt: What is one reason we learn the skill of <u>paraphrasing</u>?
Sample Answer: Being able to <u>paraphrase</u> what we read helps us better comprehend what we read.

Sample Prompt: What is another way we can use the skill of <u>paraphrasing</u>?
Sample Answer: We can <u>paraphrase</u> a writing prompt to better understand what we are being asked to do.

PRACTICE

① **Task:** Read appropriate print and online materials to research a famous monument that interests you. Take notes to <u>paraphrase</u> what you read. Follow your teacher's suggestions to list your sources. Use a separate piece of paper. 🖊

② **Task:** Determine the meaning of any words or terms that are new to you to help you when you <u>paraphrase</u> what you read.

③ **Prompt:** What did you already know about this monument before you researched it? How did this knowledge help you <u>paraphrase</u> what you read?

_____

_____

_____

_____

④ **Prompt:** Set aside the notes you took when you first <u>paraphrased</u> your research. What is something of interest you remember from your reading?

_____

_____

_____

_____

⑤ **Prompt:** Refer to your notes and write a paragraph to <u>paraphrase</u> what you learned about the monument you researched. Use a separate piece of paper.

PARAPHRASE (cont.)

☑ CHECK

Look back at what the word <u>paraphrase</u> means.

① Read the paragraph below with a small group.

The Statue of Liberty is a famous monument in the United States. The people of France gave the monument to the United States as a gift of friendship. Throughout time, the statue has held different meanings. The statue has a broken chain at its feet, which people say symbolized the end of slavery after the Civil War. Around the turn of the twentieth century, millions of immigrants came to the United States. Almost all of them entered the country by way of the New York Harbor, where they viewed the statue. It came to be a symbol of hope for the immigrants. During World Wars I and II, images of the statue encouraged people in the military as well as on the home front. This famous monument continues to stand as a symbol of freedom and democracy in the United States.

② Independently, <u>paraphrase</u> the first one or two sentences of the paragraph in writing. Use a separate piece of paper.

③ Pass your paper to the person on your right. <u>Paraphrase</u> the next one or two sentences in the paragraph.

④ Repeat step #3 until you and the other group members have completed <u>paraphrasing</u> the paragraph.

⑤ Review the paper on which you <u>paraphrased</u> the first one or two sentences. Read the ways your classmates <u>paraphrased</u> other sentences in the text.

⑥ What did you learn about <u>paraphrasing</u> from reading and discussing your classmates' writing?

_____

_____

🔍 REVIEW

- We <u>paraphrase</u> when we use different words to restate what someone says.
- When we <u>paraphrase</u> a written text, we restate the main ideas or meaning in different words.

💬 COLLABORATE

When we look back at what this word means, we see that it means to restate in different words the main idea of something said or written.

① Work with a classmate to create a T-chart, labeling one column "Paraphrasing is…" and the other column "Paraphrasing is **not**…." Use a separate piece of paper.

② Work together to complete your chart as a reference guide for <u>paraphrasing</u> what you read when you research and complete other classroom reading activities.

COMPILE

DEFINE

Question: What does it mean to <u>compile</u>?
Answer: When we <u>compile</u>, we bring together many pieces of information to create a new document. We might <u>compile</u> several short pieces into a longer written work.

STUDY

Sample Prompt: What is one reason people <u>compile</u> information about a specific topic?
Sample Answer: When people <u>compile</u> information, they can get an overview of the topic.

Sample Prompt: What is an example of how we might <u>compile</u> our writing?
Sample Answer: We might <u>compile</u> stories and poems we have written into a class book.

PRACTICE

① **Task:** Research your favorite Olympic sport or Olympic athlete. <u>Compile</u> facts and other information about that sport or athlete. Take notes on the information on a separate piece of paper. 🖊

② **Prompt:** How will you <u>compile</u> your information in a way that will be helpful to you as you write a story?

_____

_____

③ **Prompt:** Refer to the information you <u>compiled</u> to plan a story about the Olympic sport or athlete you researched. Use a web similar to the sample shown below. Within each part of your planning (characters, setting, events, problem, solution), include related details you <u>compiled</u> from your research.

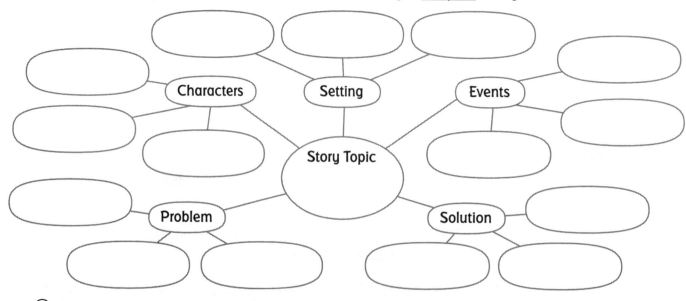

④ **Prompt:** Use a separate piece of paper to write the story you planned in Practice Prompt #3.

COMPILE (cont.)

☑ CHECK

Look back at what the word <u>compile</u> means.

① Discuss with a small group how you might <u>compile</u> the stories you wrote in Practice Prompt #4. Consider these questions:

- Which format will be best for your completed document?
- How will you organize the stories you <u>compile</u>?
- What visual elements might you include to illustrate the work you <u>compile</u>?

② Work together to <u>compile</u> your writing into a new document. Use a separate piece of paper.

③ Share your <u>compiled</u> work with the rest of the class.

🔍 REVIEW

- When we <u>compile</u>, we compose a new document using information from other sources.
- When we <u>compile</u>, we gather pieces of writing or information to create a longer written work or list.
- When we <u>compile</u>, we put together facts and information or pieces of writing into a collection.

💬 COLLABORATE

When we look back at what this word means, we see that it means to gather facts and information or pieces of writing to create a new document or collected work.

① Work with a classmate to research and <u>compile</u> data about a popular Olympic sport that has an interesting history. Use a separate piece of paper. [✐]

② How did you <u>compile</u> the data? How did you organize the information?

_____

_____

_____

③ Review the data you <u>compiled</u>.

④ Discuss with your partner what you observed from the data you <u>compiled</u>. Take notes on your discussion.

_____

_____

_____

Name: _____

CLARIFY

 DEFINE

Question: What does it mean to <u>clarify</u>?
Answer: When we <u>clarify</u>, we make something clear and easy for others to understand.

 STUDY

Sample Prompt: How can I <u>clarify</u> the meaning of coral polyps?
Sample Answer: I can look at the words and sentences nearby to get a clue to the meaning, I can ask someone, or I can use another text, such as a dictionary.

Sample Prompt: What can I do to <u>clarify</u> my understanding of what I read?
Sample Answer: I can reread a passage or stop when something doesn't make sense and think about what I've already read.

 PRACTICE

① **Task:** Read the paragraph below about coral reefs.

Coral reefs are one of Earth's most diverse and fragile ecosystems. Corals and algae live together in a symbiotic relationship that allows shallow-water corals to grow and form structures we call coral reefs. The reefs protect shorelines from storms and provide food for people and marine animals. Until recently, scientists studied coral reefs by diving to survey and observe them. NASA (National Aeronautics and Space Administration) has developed remote imaging technology to study larger expanses of coral reefs.

② **Task:** Identify any unknown words or phrases. What strategy will you use to <u>clarify</u> the meaning of those words?

_____

_____

③ **Prompt:** How would you <u>clarify</u> the explanation of a coral reef? What additional sources could you use to <u>clarify</u> your comprehension of the topic?

_____

_____

④ **Prompt:** Based on the paragraph you read and what you already know, what is an opinion you have about coral reefs? Include evidence to <u>clarify</u> your opinion and reasons for that opinion.

_____

_____

CLARIFY (cont.)

☑ CHECK

Look back at what the word <u>clarify</u> means.

① Work with a small group to discuss the health of coral-reef ecosystems. Research using print and online materials as needed. Take notes on a separate piece of paper. Consider the questions below. [!]

- What main points or factors did you identify?
- How would you <u>clarify</u> those points for readers?

② As a group, state an opinion about the health of coral-reef ecosystems.

③ What reasons and details would help <u>clarify</u> the stated opinion for readers?

④ Work together to ask and answer questions about the topic to <u>clarify</u> your understanding of the topic. Use a separate piece of paper.

✎ REVIEW

- When we <u>clarify</u>, we clear up any confusion about something.
- When we <u>clarify</u> something, we make it easier for others to understand.

💬 COLLABORATE

When we look back at what this word means, we see that it means to make something clear and easy to understand.

① Work with a classmate to discuss the writing prompt below.

Think about the role coral reefs play in an ocean ecosystem. How would you explain the relationships between coral-reef organisms and other marine animals?

② How would you rewrite the prompt to <u>clarify</u> what it is asking you to do?

_____

_____

_____

_____

_____

③ Work with your partner to create a graphic organizer to <u>clarify</u> the writing prompt in #1 above. Use a separate piece of paper.

Name: _____

REVISE

 DEFINE

Question: What does it mean to <u>revise</u>?
Answer: When we <u>revise</u>, we change or correct something. We might <u>revise</u> something to make it different.

 STUDY

Sample Prompt: Why do we <u>revise</u> our writing?
Sample Answer: We want to make our writing as clear and easy for readers to understand as possible.

Sample Prompt: What are things we can do to strengthen writing when we <u>revise</u> it?
Sample Answer: We can make sure the opinion or focus is clearly stated and that reasons and examples support the main idea. We can make sure word choices reflect exactly what we want to say.

 PRACTICE

① **Task:** Read the paragraph below and think about how it could be <u>revised</u> to strengthen the writing. Use a separate piece of paper to answer Practice Prompts #2–#4 below.

Even though volcanoes pose a risk, millions of people live near these unpredictable landforms. Technology enables scientists to study volcanic activity. They observe magma and seismic pressure. Predicting the next eruption, however, is less exact. Volcanoes become famous as we study and learn about their potential for destruction. Mount Vesuvius in Italy has erupted more than thirty times since a major eruption occurred nearly two thousand years ago. The eruption buried two cities under ash and mudslides. Now over four million people live within an area that could be destroyed if another major eruption occurs.

② **Prompt:** How might you <u>revise</u> the paragraph to include visual elements that would increase reader comprehension?

③ **Prompt:** What additional facts and details could you include to <u>revise</u> and strengthen the paragraph?

④ **Prompt:** How would you <u>revise</u> the concluding statement to strengthen the paragraph?

⑤ **Prompt:** On a separate piece of paper, write an informative paragraph about a volcano you have researched. Think about a unique focus and purpose for your paragraph. 🖊

⑥ **Prompt:** How might you <u>revise</u> your writing to include precise or vivid words that explain your topic?

_____

_____

_____

_____

REVISE *(cont.)*

☑ CHECK

Look back at what the word <u>revise</u> means.

① Observe as your teacher models how to <u>revise</u> a sample sentence about volcanoes. 🖊

② Participate in a class discussion about what it means to <u>revise</u> and what you noticed when your teacher modeled <u>revising</u> one sentence.

③ Discuss with classmates how you could use technology to <u>revise</u> writing before publishing it.

④ Read the paragraph below with classmates.

Mount Sinabung, a volcano in Indonesia, has had multiple eruptions in recent years. More than one eruption has caused deaths and injuries. Authorities have evacuated thousands of families from a danger zone near the volcano. Eruptions have included flows of fragmented volcanic rock, ash plumes, and avalanches. Scientists monitored seismic activity and growth of the lava dome during the eruption period.

⑤ What changes would you make to <u>revise</u> the paragraph?

_____

_____

_____

⑥ Work with classmates to <u>revise</u> the paragraph to reflect a different perspective or point of view. Use a separate piece of paper.

🔍 REVIEW

- We <u>revise</u> something when we change or correct it.
- We can <u>revise</u> something by making it different.
- When we <u>revise</u>, we think about what we might add to strengthen our writing.
- When we <u>revise</u>, we think about word choice and take out extra words.

💬 COLLABORATE

When we look back at what this word means, we see that it means to change writing to strengthen it or make it correct.

① With a classmate, discuss possible audiences for the informative paragraphs you wrote for Practice Prompt #5.

② How might you <u>revise</u> your writing to make it more interesting for readers?

_____

_____

Name: _____

INFER/MAKE AN INFERENCE

 DEFINE

Question: What does it mean to <u>infer</u>? How do we <u>make an inference</u>?
Answer: When we <u>infer</u>, we draw a conclusion after considering all the facts. We <u>make an inference</u> when we use evidence along with what we already know to draw a conclusion.

 STUDY

Sample Prompt: Based on what you already know, what would you <u>infer</u> people use a gold pan for?
Sample Answer: I know you can put liquids and solids in a pan, so I would <u>infer</u> that people use a gold pan to lift sediment out of the creek water and spread it out to find gold.

Sample Prompt: What can you <u>infer</u> if you read a story about mining for gold?
Sample Answer: I already know that in the past, people mined for gold. I would <u>infer</u> that in a story about mining for gold, people might go to a place where they think they would find this valuable metal.

✏️ **PRACTICE**

① **Prompt:** What do you already know about gold rushes?

_____

_____

_____

② **Task:** Read the paragraph below.

The California Gold Rush of the 1800s made history. But it's still possible to mine for gold in the creeks of California in current times. In 2017, the state experienced an unusually wet winter. Heavy storms and increased rainfall uprooted trees, caused erosion, and changed the landscape. The resulting flooding and runoff carried additional sediment from mountains into lower-elevation creeks. The force of the storm runoff shook loose mineral deposits from mines and riverbeds. It also washed out known gold digs. Geologists say the erosion removed surface soil and light rock, exposing gold veins that haven't been visible for two hundred years.

③ **Prompt:** <u>Make an inference</u> about the new gold rush. Connect two or more details from the text above to what you already know about the topic as indicated in your response to Practice Prompt #1.

_____

_____

_____

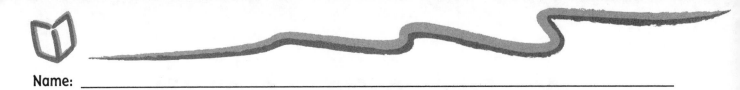

Name: _____

INFER/MAKE AN INFERENCE *(cont.)*

☑ CHECK

Look back at what the word <u>infer</u> means. Think about what it means to <u>make an inference</u>.

① Work with a small group to create a three-column chart to observe how we <u>make an inference</u>. Use a separate piece of paper. Label the left column of your chart "What I Know." Label the center column of the chart "Evidence." Label the right column with the word "Inference."

② Take turns writing what you know about the topic of mining for gold in the left column of the chart.

③ In your group, review the paragraph in the Practice section or read additional information about mining for gold as available. Discuss details and evidence in the text you read that added to your understanding of the topic. Write your observations in the center column of the chart. 🖊

④ What can you <u>infer</u> from your knowledge and the evidence in the text? Write what you <u>infer</u> on a separate piece of paper.

⑤ Discuss what you <u>inferred</u> in #4 with others in your group. Work together to complete the third column of the chart.

🔍 REVIEW

- When we <u>infer</u>, we come to a conclusion based on facts and logical reasons.
- We can use evidence in a text along with what we already know about a topic to <u>make an inference</u> about what the author wants to say.
- We use facts and what we know to <u>infer</u> something that is not directly stated.

💬 COLLABORATE

When we look back at what <u>infer</u> and <u>make an inference</u> mean, we see that they mean to use facts and previous knowledge to draw a conclusion.

① With a classmate, review the paragraph in the Practice section or use another selection about a new gold rush from available print or online materials. 🖊

② Model for your partner how you can <u>make an inference</u> about a new gold rush. Place one or more sticky notes next to the evidence in the text you used to <u>make an inference</u>. Discuss with your partner what you <u>inferred</u> about the text.

③ What questions did you ask about the text to <u>make an inference</u> about what the author wanted to say?

_____

_____

ACADEMIC CONCEPTS GLOSSARY

On the activity pages, you may read some words that are new to you. This glossary has definitions for words you will see in the writing prompts and tasks. Always keep a copy of this glossary on hand as you complete each activity page.

academic (adj.) – having to do with study and learning

accomplishment (n.) – something that is done successfully

anonymous (adj.) – written, done, or given by a person whose name is not known or made public

argument (n.) – a person's opinion about something

argumentative (adj.) – a type of writing that presents an argument

article (n.) – a piece of writing published in a newspaper or magazine

aspect (n.) – one feature or characteristic of something

audience (n.) – the people who read a published piece of writing or who listen to a presentation

author (n.) – the writer of a story, book, article, play, or poem

bibliography (n.) – a list of resources an author used to research a topic

biographical (adj.) – about someone's life story

brochure (n.) – a booklet, usually with pictures, that gives information about something

capitalization (n.) – the use of capital letters in writing or printing

caption (n.) – a short title or description printed with a drawing or photograph

category (n.) – a class or group of things that have something in common

cause (n.) – the reason that something happens

character (n.) – one of the people (or an animal, creature, etc.) in a story, book, or play

characteristic (n.) – a quality or feature

chart (n.) – a drawing that shows information in the form of a table, graph, or picture

circumstances (n.) – the facts or conditions connected with an event

collage (n.) – a picture made by attaching different things to a surface

conclusion (n.) – the end of a story, article, or other piece of writing

concrete (adj.) – real or definite

connection (n.) – a link between people, objects, or ideas

constructive (adj.) – helpful and useful, as in *constructive criticism*

content (n.) – the topic, important parts, or meaning of a book or other written or spoken work

conventions (n.) – the usual rules we follow to write English correctly

criteria (n.) – standards on which a judgment or decision may be based

ACADEMIC CONCEPTS GLOSSARY *(cont.)*

data (n.) – information or facts

debate (n.) – a discussion between sides with different views

decision (n.) – something you have made up your mind about

definition (n.) – an explanation of the meaning of a word or phrase

design (n.) – the shape or style of something

detail (n.) – a small part of a whole item

diagram (n.) – a drawing or plan that explains something

diction (n.) – the clearness of a person's speech or the way in which words are used in speech or writing

dictionary (n.) – a book that lists words in alphabetical order and explains what they mean

directions (n.) – instructions on how to do something; orders on what to do

discovery (n.) – something that is found or found out about

discussion (n.) – a conversation about a topic to better understand it

document (n.) – a piece of paper containing important information

effect (n.) – the result or consequence of something

effective (adj.) – working very well

element (n.) – one of the simple, basic parts of something

essay (n.) – a piece of writing about a particular subject

evidence (n.) – information and facts that help prove something or make a person believe something is true

excerpt (n.) – a short piece taken from a longer piece of writing, music, or film

expert (n.) – someone who is very skilled in something or who knows a lot about a particular subject

explanation (n.) – the reason for something that makes it clear why it happened

expository (adj.) – a type of writing that explains something

factor (n.) – one of the things that helps produce a result

feature (n.) – an important part or quality of something

feedback (n.) – comments and reactions to something

fiction (n.) – stories about characters and events that are not real

figurative language (n.) – words or expressions that have a meaning that is different from the literal interpretation

figure of speech (n.) – an expression in which words are used in a colorful or poetic way

findings (n.) – the results of an investigation or study

fluency (n.) – the ability to speak or write smoothly and clearly

focus (n.) – the center of activity, interest, or attention

graphic organizer (n.) – a visual display to explain how facts, terms, or ideas are connected to each other

graphics (n.) – images such as drawings, maps, or graphs

informational text (n.) – nonfiction writing that informs readers about a topic

insight (n.) – an understanding about a matter or person that is not obvious

instructions (n.) – directions on how to do something; orders on what to do

interaction (n.) – the action between people, groups, or things

investigation (n.) – an observation or study by close examination to learn facts or information about someone or something

issue (n.) – a main topic for debate

journal entry (n.) – an individual piece of writing that allows someone to express his or her feelings and opinions

judgment (n.) – an opinion of something or someone

key word (n.) – a word or concept of great significance

literature group (n.) – a group of students who studies a particular piece of writing

logical (adj.) – careful and correct reasoning or thinking about something

materials (n.) – things used in doing a particular activity

meaningful (adj.) – having a meaning or purpose; expressing an emotion or idea without words; having real importance or value

media (n.) – the means for communicating information to large numbers of people

memorable (adj.) – easily remembered or worth remembering

mental (adj.) – to do with or done by the mind

motive (n.) – a reason for doing something

multimedia (adj.) – using or involving several forms of communication or expression

narrative (n.) – a story or an account of something that has happened

narrator (n.) – the person who tells a story

nonfiction (n.) – writing that is not fiction, especially information about real people, things, places, and events

nuance (n.) – a subtle distinction or variation; a very small difference in meaning

online (adj.) – connected to, or available from, a system of computers, such as the Internet

opinion (n.) – the ideas and beliefs a person has about something

option (n.) – something that you can choose to do

ACADEMIC CONCEPTS GLOSSARY *(cont.)*

outline (n.) – the basic points or ideas about something

paragraph (n.) – a short passage that is about a single subject or idea

passage (n.) – a short section in a book or other piece of writing

peer (n.) – a person of the same age or standing as another

phrase (n.) – a group of words that have meaning but do not form a sentence

poem (n.) – a piece of writing arranged in short lines, often with a rhythm and some words that rhyme

point of view (n.) – an attitude, a viewpoint, or a way of looking at something

precise (adj.) – very correct or exact

preliminary (adj.) – preparing the way for something important that comes later

presentation (n.) – an activity in which someone shows, describes, or explains something to a group of people

problem (n.) – a difficult situation that needs to be figured out or overcome

procedure (n.) – a way of doing something, often consisting of a series of steps

process (n.) – an organized series of actions that produce a result

prompt (n.) – text that asks a person to do something or provide information

punctuation mark (n.) – a written mark, such as a comma, period, or question mark, used to make the meaning of writing clear

quality (n.) – a special characteristic of someone or something

quotation (n.) – a sentence or short passage from a book, play, or speech that is repeated by someone else

reaction (n.) – an action in response to something

recently (adv.) – describing something that happened, was made, or done a short time ago

recipient (n.) – a person who receives something

reference materials (n.) – printed or online information used to study and learn about a topic

relationship (n.) – the way in which things or people are connected

resolution (n.) – an answer or solution to something, such as a conflict or problem

resource (n.) – something valuable or useful to a place or person; something that you can go to for help

response (n.) – a reply or answer to something; a reaction

result (n.) – something that happens because of something else

role (n.) – the job or purpose of a person or thing; the part that a person acts in a play

rubric (n.) – a guide listing specific criteria for scoring academic papers or projects

sample (n.) – a small amount of something that shows what the whole is like

ACADEMIC CONCEPTS GLOSSARY (cont.)

scene (n.) – a part of a story, play, or movie that shows what is happening in one particular place and time

segment (n.) – a part or section of something

sensory (adj.) – of or relating to your physical senses

sequence (n.) – a series or collection of things that follow in order

setting (n.) – the place where and time when a story takes place

simile (n.) – a way of describing something by comparing it with something else, using the word *like* or *as* to compare the two things

sketch (n.) – a quick, rough drawing of something

solution (n.) – the answer or explanation to a problem

source (n.) – the place, person, or thing from which something comes

specific (adj.) – something exact or individually named

spelling (n.) – the way in which a word is correctly formed using letters

structure (n.) – the way something is put together or organized

summary (n.) – a short statement that gives the main ideas of something that has been said or written

table (n.) – a chart that lists facts and figures, usually in columns

table of contents (n.) – a list of titles of the parts of a book, listed in the order the parts appear in the book

technology (n.) – the use of science and engineering to do practical things

text (n.) – the main section of writing in a book, other than the pictures, glossary, or index

theme (n.) – the main subject or idea of a piece of writing or talk

thesaurus (n.) – a book that lists words in alphabetical order and gives related words that have the same and opposite meanings

tone (n.) – a way of speaking or writing that shows a certain feeling or attitude

topic (n.) – the subject of a discussion, study, lesson, speech, or piece of writing

trait (n.) – a quality or characteristic that makes one thing different from another

version (n.) – one description or account given from a particular point of view

visual aid (n.) – something you look at (such as a chart) that is used to make something easier to understand

vocabulary (n.) – the words that a person uses and understands

website (n.) – a group of linked computer files on the World Wide Web

LEXILE MEASURES

The Lexile® measures for the texts are listed in the table below. For reference, see the key that follows. It lists the Typical Reader Measures by grade level, as well as the Typical Text Measures by grade level.

Verb	Text	Page # in Book	Lexile® Measure
Collaborate	Practice Task #1	8	840L
Report	Practice Task #1	10	930L
Plan	Practice Task #1	20	860L
Argue	Check #1	25	1070L
Apply	Practice Task #1	32	910L
Categorize	Collaborate #1	37	930L
Predict	Practice Task #1	38	820L
Conclude/Draw a Conclusion	Collaborate #1	41	940L
Question	Practice Task #1	50	930L
Analyze	Practice Task #1	56	740L
Criticize	Check #1	65	930L
Incorporate	Collaborate #1	67	1030L
Distinguish	Collaborate #1	73	870L
Draft	Collaborate #1	83	1000L
Edit	Practice Task #2	84	860L
Summarize	Check #1	91	960L
Paraphrase	Check #1	95	910L
Clarify	Practice Task #1	98	1200L
Revise	Practice Task #1	100	970L
Revise	Check #4	101	1020L
Infer/Make an Inference	Practice Task #2	102	980L

REFERENCE KEY: TYPICAL MEASURE RANGES FOR GRADE 5

Typical Reader Measure	Typical Text Measure (Text Demand Study, 2009)	Typical Text Measure (CCSS, 2012)
565L to 910L	730L to 850L	830L to 1010L

MEETING STANDARDS

Each lesson meets one or more of the following Common Core State Standards © Copyright 2010. National Governors Association Center for Best Practices and Council of Chief State School Officers. All rights reserved. For more information about the Common Core State Standards, go to *http://www.corestandards.org/* or *http://www.teachercreated.com/standards/.*

Reading: Literature	Lesson
Key Ideas and Details	
ELA.RL.5.1: Quote accurately from a text when explaining what the text says explicitly and when drawing inferences from the text.	Contrast, Analyze, Criticize, Draft, Recite
ELA.RL.5.2: Determine a theme of a story, drama, or poem from details in the text, including how characters in a story or drama respond to challenges or how the speaker in a poem reflects upon a topic; summarize the text.	Contrast, Predict, Analyze, Criticize, Summarize, Recite
ELA.RL.5.3: Compare and contrast two or more characters, settings, or events in a story or drama, drawing on specific details in the text (e.g., how characters interact).	Contrast, Predict, Analyze, Criticize
Craft and Structure	
ELA.RL.5.5: Explain how a series of characters, scenes, or stanzas fits together to provide the overall structure of a particular story, drama, or poem.	Analyze, Criticize
ELA.RL.5.6: Describe how a narrator's or speaker's point of view influences how events are described.	Predict, Draft
Integration of Knowledge and Ideas	
ELA.RL.5.9: Compare and contrast stories in the same genre (e.g., mysteries and adventure stories) on their approaches to similar themes and topics.	Contrast

Reading: Informational Text	Lesson
Key Ideas and Details	
ELA.RI.5.1: Quote accurately from a text when explaining what the text says explicitly and when drawing inferences from the text.	Explain, Plan, Argue, Contrast, Apply, Defend, Cite, Analyze, Incorporate, Distinguish, Summarize, Compile, Infer/Make an Inference
ELA.RI.5.2: Determine two or more main ideas of a text and explain how they are supported by key details; summarize the text.	Report, Explain, Apply, Categorize, Conclude/Draw a Conclusion, Defend, Analyze, Incorporate, Summarize, Paraphrase
ELA.RI.5.3: Explain the relationships or interactions between two or more individuals, events, ideas, or concepts in a historical, scientific, or technical text based on specific information in the text.	Report, Explain, Plan, Contrast, Apply, Categorize, Question, Analyze, Incorporate, Distinguish, Paraphrase, Compile, Clarify, Infer/Make an Inference
Craft and Structure	
ELA.RI.5.4: Determine the meaning of general academic and domain-specific words and phrases in a text relevant to a *grade 5 topic or subject area.*	Explain, Argue, Contrast, Apply, Categorize, Question, Edit, Clarify
ELA.RI.5.5: Compare and contrast the overall structure (e.g., chronology, comparison, cause/effect, problem/solution) of events, ideas, concepts, or information in two or more texts.	Contrast, Analyze
ELA.RI.5.6: Analyze multiple accounts of the same event or topic, noting important similarities and differences in the point of view they represent.	Analyze